Who Stole My Energy?

Renee Henderson

Guardian House

Who Stole My Energy?
by Renee Henderson

ISBN: 978-0-9941119-4-4   Paperback
Henderson, Renee, 1969-
Who Stole My Energy? / Renee Henderson.
North Island, New Zealand
Originally Published: 2016.

Published in 2016 by Guardian House
www.guardianhouse.tumblr.com
AUCKLAND, NEW ZEALAND

CAUTION: The information given in this book is not intended to act
as a substitute for medical treatment, nor can it be used for
diagnosis

Who Stole My Energy?

Renee Henderson

Guardian House

About the Author

The Castles we live in today, were first built in the air... live your dreams.   – Renee Henderson

Renee Henderson is a writer, author, growth consultant, teacher and profiler. She is also a Photographer, Contemporary Abstract Artist, Digital Artist. Renee is an international writer and author here are some of her book titles:

- How to Read and Influence People

- Who Stole My Energy?

- You Can Transform Your Life

- Social Media for the Soul Vol. 1

- Wisdom
  - Wisdom of Nature
  - Wisdom of Children

- The Healing Art
  Contemporary Art, Photography, Digital Art.

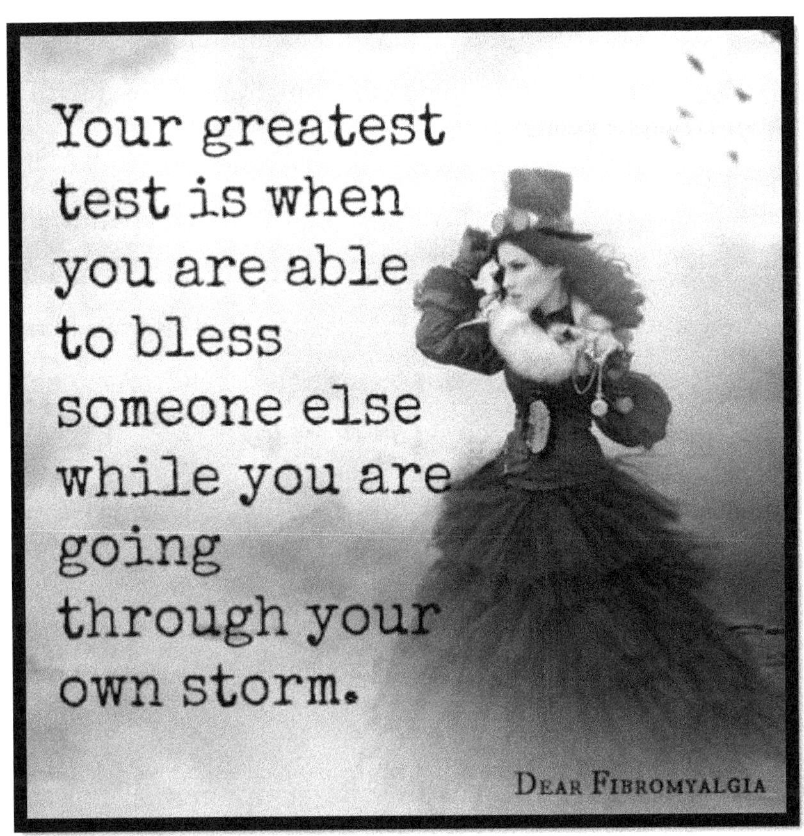

Renee would like to thank you for allowing her to share her knowledge and experiences with you, and she also thanks you for allowing her to share her story here with all of you while she is going through her own storm and learning and growing from her storm, as she is sure we all do.

Even through the following obstacles Renee continues her work as a consultant, teacher, profiler, writer/author and more. If you wish to do something you find a way, if you don't wish to do something you will always find excuses.

Renee writes to share insights, understanding and compassion, that she hopes will continue to be shared with the Readers friends, family, partners or share even in business.

Renee lives with Fibromyalgia and severe pain daily. Fibromyalgia can be an extremely painful and exhausting condition, and for some it can cause disability. Renee likes to educate people about this invisible syndrome called Fibromyalgia and make people more aware.

What is Fibromyalgia? Try to imagine the last time you had the flu. The aches and pains, stiffness, headaches, feeling drained of energy, unable to get a decent night's sleep, unable to concentrate, discomfort, and at times just a completely unpleasant experience.

Now try to imagine having these flu symptoms all the time, and with all over muscle pain as a permanent constant. This will give you an idea of what it is like to have Fibromyalgia on a good day. Finding a way to manage her Fibromyalgia and improving on her own health and well-being, Renee began her journey toward understanding more about herself and then others.

Learning about emotional behaviour and human behaviour, and about the energy that can either help or hinder us, which then lead Renee to further understanding, but it also made her very sensitive to energy and the energy of others.

This new found sensitivity gave her more clarity and magnified her senses, now Renee is able to see more clearly how understanding energy more could help not only herself but others in all areas of their lives. Being this sensitive made it so much easier for Renee to read another person's energy, and learn further about what knowledge they required to achieve their sought after goals.

Also over her many years she has lived with and manage being diagnosed with severe and sometimes crippling depression. Renee hopes that through her work as a writer, author she would motivate and inspire others to create a life for themselves where they may have once thought there was none due to health or lifestyle issues that they once thought they could not overcome.

Renee also continues her journey of writing as through her work she continues to unmask even more understandings into herself and into other people in aid of helping herself and in hopes of being of some help to other people in need and offer some relief and benefit to those who are seeking further understanding, help and healing.

Through her journey of awareness, understanding emotions, energy, feelings, human behaviour, intuitive energy, transformation and change and more, Renee has gained benefits and healing to help manage her own life and health and she is not done yet as she considers herself a work in progress. Renee believes everyone has something to teach and everyone has something to learn, it does not matter who we are or where we are in life we can all help one another even in some small way, even if it is leading by our own example.

Renee has learnt that whatever is written in a book, be it any book, including this one, that it is only one translation and only one person's opinion, and so Renee writes not to give you something to believe in, but to offer you another point of view so you can go away and form your very own beliefs. There are no beliefs that are completely true and that is why we all continue to search for further answers and understanding and continue to learn and grow and nurture ourselves and our souls in this process.

Renee ask that you please not be offended by any views or writings that you read, and just to remember this is only to provoke awareness and thought, and to provoke further growth of yourself and your soul. This is an opportunity to see life from a different point of view and then create your own views. We are all here to help each other, and we may not agree with one another all the time but at least we can open our minds and then maybe open our hearts to others views so that understanding can be gained and from these understandings, compassion may grow and create a healing that our world so desperately needs.

If you would like to know what is right in your life, or right in this world, you simply have to ask what is hurting yourself or someone else and what is not hurting another. That should give you the path that many should take, and yet so many take the path of hurting another, and no healing can come from this, and it is such a simple message. And have you ever noticed that the questions you may be asking tend to have the simplest of solutions and the simplest of answers.

If parents allowed it children asked many questions and some parents may have thought their child an old soul, not an old soul, the children just asked questions which brought on growth. We have to stop and ask ourselves why we stop asking so many questions. We have to also stop and ask why we decided to stop growing by no longer asking so many questions.

Renee hopes that the understandings that she shares will inspire and motivate a change, a healing and a transformation in others and in our world today.

Everything we hear is an opinion, not a fact

everything we see is a perspective not the truth.

- Marcus Aurelius

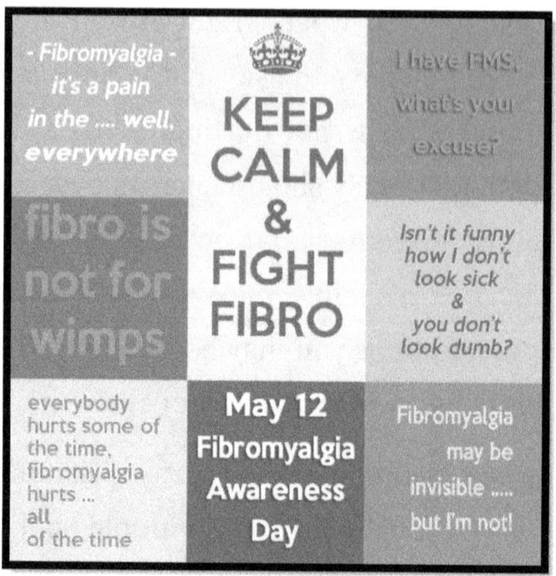

By your thoughts, by your beliefs, by your imagination, by your will, you create, guide, and maintain your life.

You are the creator of the movie of your life. Nothing happens by accident or chance, it is all cause and effect. If cause was sown during a past frame of your life-movie, when the effect comes along it is seen as either good or bad luck, chance, coincidence, or an accident. Time separates!

Despite appearances, life does not work in this manner. You shape and mould the life you live. You create your fortune and misfortune. It is a good idea to remember this, and apply it to your ongoing moment.

-Michael J. Roads, The Oracle

Contents

Introduction

This book is about taking a refreshing view of your life through my eyes, as a flowing of energy – in and out. Energy is your life force and this is about understanding it and having control over it, because if you don't have control over it, then you are going to always be full of the wrong sort of energy.

The tools of awareness and understanding are simple tools that if you can master, (and I am sure you will master) will give you power and control over your own life and therefore give you back your energy. With newfound clarity you can see if you are actually heading in the right direction, or going backwards instead of forwards in life. When you read you will see what you want to see, because this is all about you; no one but you can heal you. Only you have the power to do so. When you are ill, it is your choice to take yourself to a doctor or not. It is your choice to read the words within these pages – a personal decision.

The lessons that come from *Who Stole My Energy?* can give you new insights, less tension in your body, a healthier you and may even help you to feel lighter and clearer about you and where you are going. When you learn how to take back your power and control you will be able to attain your personal and professional goals. With personal life goals you may gain a healthier and fitter you, the career or relationship you really want and a life you may never have thought about or dreamed possible.

Knowledge contains the tools, and *Who Stole My Energy?* is about giving you more tools to work with to help you improve your existing life or lifestyle and gain personal well-being. It is about truly knowing yourself and being empowered. *Who Stole My Energy?* may challenge your beliefs – push some of your boundaries – by making you think about what was, what is and what will come. You may recognize your own hidden beliefs. Take only what you want; what helps you.

Certain points recur throughout the book so that they stick with you. The message can't get lost among the words. You should see and hear it clearly enough so it sticks. *Who Stole My Energy?* may even irritate you, trigger you into an emotional response and if it does, good. That means it is working and you are beginning to move years of blocks. If you become triggered, upset, see it as an opportunity to heal a suppressed block or past experience you have hung onto; you may not even have realized it.

What you dream about is not always impossible. People may scoff at the others who build castles in the air, but many of us are living in those very castles today, so live your dreams. The only thing standing between your present life and the life you would love to lead is you. *Who Stole My Energy?* is all about helping you live the life you want and tells you how to get it. What happened to you in the past, present and what will happen to you in the future is all within your control, your power.

Who Stole My Energy? is about returning you to your true power. I can only show you the gateway to your life, your true life, the one you were born to live, but you are the one who has to walk through the gateway.

You may feel that it is your destiny to help others. We are all here to help one another. But I would suggest you read and understand the content of *Who Stole My Energy?* and start by using it to empower yourself before you try to rush out and help others. Gain insights into yourself first. The old adages; a little knowledge is a dangerous thing and we must first learn to walk before we can run apply here. Integrate the knowledge within these pages into your own life first and then run with it. Talk to your neighbor or a friend. Sharing what you know is free, and only takes a moment. You may find you have helped them more than you know.

You are your greatest teacher and guru but you are also the student. *Who Stole My Energy?* gives you the tools to continue to learn from yourself, your greatest resource. Then when you fall in life, your newfound knowledge allows you to recognize the fact and gives you the choice of whether or not to pick yourself up, whereas before you may never have even known you fell and just stayed down there in your rut.

Who Stole My Energy? is not about changing your beliefs, but about strengthening your present beliefs or even helping you create your own set of beliefs. It is adding to your already vast knowledge and life experience, giving strength and power to your personal life foundation. The stronger the life foundation, the more chance you give yourself to succeed.

Throughout this book I have shared many quotes; a little more wisdom to gain from. It is my hope that each time you pick up this book and open it to read or re-read you gain yet another new insight; more knowledge to have at your fingertips which to help you along on your life journey.

The teacher sought a holy man who had left this worldliness of life behind to enter seclusion in a cave; there to find perfect peace. Though the teacher had traveled far up a mountain to find this holy man, he wasn't happy to be found. When the teacher talked to him, the holy man, who had been in silence for the past 20 years, was startled.

"What is it you want?" he asked.

"I want to know why you've come all the way up here," the teacher inquired.

With a slight look of pride on his face, the holy man said, "I came here to find perfect peace."

"How foolish!" the teacher laughed. "Men like us can never find that."

The holy man rose, stared at his visitor, and bellowed, "How dare you come and disturb my meditation with this! Get out of here this instant!"

The teacher stood up and looked him in the eye. "Where is the perfect peace you sought now?" he asked. "Come down the hill with me, and I'll teach you how to have what you seek."

The holy man left his mountaintop, and on the walk down to the village, became enlightened.

—Daniel Levin, *The Zen Book.*

Energy is inside us and all around us and yet we are not aware of energy and the huge role it plays in our lives.

Energy is the invisible glue that holds everything together or tears everything down or in some cases tears people apart from the inside out, which is not pretty for anyone and it does affect everyone.

We need to learn as much as we can about energy so we know exactly what we are working with and how to get energy to work for us instead of against us. Do not think for a moment that you can get through life without knowledge of energy as that would be unwise, do you really want to work harder in life for little results or would you like to work smarter and achieve more of what you have only wish for and only spoke of this wish in a whisper to yourself. What we wish for can be achieved through understanding energy a lot more than you do presently, let energy reward you, and give you what you wish for without judgment it is your choice.

Energy is invisible as is the air and gravity and yet we believe in air and gravity because we have learnt about them. So too is energy like air and gravity and I ask you to begin a journey into learning about energy as part of your journey to transformation of you and your life.

Many believe in God and yet no one has met God face to face in our life time that I know of, those who study religion believe in God and that God created everything. We believe in God, fight wars over one God, we go to churches, temples and other places of worship to pray and continue our study of God and yet no one has seen God and yet many believe including myself. If you can believe in God then learning and believing in energy will be an easy step and do remember God gave us energy to help us along our life paths.

I believe in God, and I have studied many faiths and religions, not just one and keeping an open mind. People attack you if you are not this or that religion and there should be no fighting or war over God. As God is a beautiful energy of love and of creation, not one of fear, control and destruction. The message here is use the energy that God gave us to gain a much easier and lighter path to travel, where the road rises up to meet you instead of you looking for the path through the clutter and finding this task difficult. Let this reward from God which is Energy be used in positive and loving ways.

We hold so much power inside us and all around us in the form of energy. I am not going to ask you to go on blind faith throughout these pages I will give you proof that energy is not only real but used in the right way can assist you in gaining transformation and success in life and much more.

Children are more sensitive to energy and as we grow we soon let go of our sensitivity and it just is set aside and soon forgotten about. That sensitivity is a gift that with learning about energy we hope to reignite so that you can achieve so much more.

Energy is like fuel for our body, just as food is and many now days eat a diet of junk food as in food and the same with energy people create and live with so much energy junk foods and I am here hoping to change that, but in the end you are the only person who can say I am ready to take that step and make the choice to learn about energy and create transformation in your life and more energy for life.

You may feel the ripple effects of energy in your life and not even know about it, and maybe just think this is the hand life has given me and I have to play it well it doesn't have to be that way at all.

Take for instance holistic pulsing which is a body work based on pulsing the body, or the way a mother will gently rock her baby to sleep that is what I was taught holistic pulsing was based on. When using Holistic Pulsing on an adult, the bigger the pulse the more you feel it and know what is happening. The slower or gentler the pulsing the more powerful the internal release and the more relaxed you become and the more you benefit that is if you have prepared yourself for this release. If you are not aware of the internal releases that will come when an Earthquakes occurs then you are in for a bumpy ride and worse.

Recently, in Christchurch, New Zealand (September 2010) they experienced a 7.1 Earthquake and if memory serves they had over 270 aftershocks averaging 5.4 and counting. Like Holistic Pulsing the bigger the pulse the more you feel it and know that it is happening and you will not have that much of an internal release as you would with a slower and gentler pulsing action. What the rest of New Zealand and surrounding smaller islands did not realize was all those people across the board would have been affected by the gentle pulsing (if you will) and would not of been prepared for the release that came from the Earthquake that was miles away from them or the effect of the energy from the shifting plates below New Zealand that continued long after the Earthquake and aftershocks had finished.

Makes you look at Earthquakes very differently and those you have trained or received Holistic Pulsing may gain a little more insight. Holistic Pulsing can release energy blocked when it should be flowing, it can release medications and such that you have taken and clear your system of this and more and that is why it is so important to drink plenty of water after receiving a session of holistic pulsing.

What I share here is only one way of explaining the true power that energy has on us, be it inside or all around us or internally. Energy is power and they say knowledge is power so knowledge of energy and its impact and uses can you imagine the power that comes with that one, that is very powerful indeed!

Chapter 1   Energy is Life

Until you can understand that nothing can happen to you, nothing can ever come to you or be kept from you, except in accord with your state of consciousness, you do not have the key to life.

—Paul Twitchell, *The Flute of God (Eckankar)*.

From the book A Guide for the Advance Soul.

Susan Hayward.

The word 'energy' is interpreted in so many different ways, so to start let's define how I use it in the context of this book. Energy is all around us, and inside us. We are energy and everything is energy, though we take it for granted. Energy is always moving – forward or backwards – and is never still.

Take breathing for example; we breathe in and out all day, every day yet we rarely notice this simple action.

Right now, are you breathing deeply, taking shallow breaths, or worse, are you holding your breath? How do you breathe on a daily basis? How were you breathing yesterday? I am sure you really have to think to answer. Can you imagine trying to remember to breathe every second of every day? Our breath flows into and out of us every day. We don't think about it yet if we stopped breathing we would stop living.

Energy is like breath. It too, flows into and out of us every day and if your energy got too low in your body you would no longer live. Energy is life. Your personal energy is your life force, a source of power that everyone has access to.

We are all part of the same energy, and so we actually are all on equal footing. I have had people say to me that they would like to be more like me, and I say they are. Maybe you know someone you want to be like as well. All you need to do is clear away the clutter in your life and mind to find yourself standing right beside them.

Understanding what I will share with you will give you the tools to clear away the clutter in your life. Then you will see we are all standing beside one another.

Understanding energy, how it works, and how much control you have over your own energy is an important step to building a solid life foundation upon which to build a better life. If you have not built a strong foundation and on this you build your life, you will later see the cracks show. Everything may collapse around you and leave you standing there wondering how it happened.

In terms of energy, we are both predator and prey. We are, by nature, predators for energy, and so we find ways to get energy. But then we are also prey for everyone else's demands for our energy. We actually feed off each other's energy or life force. We give energy away without realizing it and we take it back in many different forms, some not so nice. Understanding and awareness allows you to give and receive energy healthily.

Why strive to give and receive energy healthily? I am sure you have heard sayings like, you get back what you give out, or you reap what you sow. If you give out healthy energy your mind and life is cleared of clutter, your path through life becomes a little easier, and you start to receive what you want and need. Give out unhealthy energy and your life becomes more clouded and darker. You can't see for looking, and opportunities seem to be blocked. Then you are left standing there asking; 'Why is this always happening to me? Why me? Life is so unfair to me!'

The truth is, nothing happens to you without you asking for it with your energy.

I spoke to a lady once and she had been in a little accident she was busily blaming others for. It couldn't possibly be her fault. I asked her why she thought it happened to her. She didn't know the answer. I asked her if she was negative toward herself or others. She replied that she was negative toward herself, a lot. I already knew she was negative toward herself but she had to say it, to own it, to be aware of what she does. Being aware of the negative energy is a step toward healing that area of her life. It turned out that she'd been negative toward herself for a long time. When we put out any energy, as a rule it must come back in that form. Negative energy comes back as negative energy. She had put out so much negative energy that it had come back to her in the form of an accident. It could have been much worse for her.

Consider the idea that in the universe around you there are mirrors everywhere that reflect not only the environment but the energies from the beings in that environment. In this example, imagine that you get angry because your son, who is overseas in Peru climbing mountains, hasn't written to you in six weeks and you are feeling really miserable and angry about it. Even the late morning's mail didn't bring anything and you had held your breath waiting till then. You may have then even voiced this to your daughter who lives down the street. Although your son may not be aware of your anger, you have still put out a number of negative thoughts. This negativity bounces off those mirrors and comes back to you. Not just from one mirror, but from a number of them. This reaction may start off as something small like you spill the milk while making yourself a cup of coffee – no big deal really – but because you're already angry it seems worse. Then a neighbour drops in to say hello and before you know it you've bitten her head off, when all she wanted was to trim the hedge between you and you thought she was having a go at you. As the day wears on other similar incidents happen that serve only to make you feel worse, and cause your negativity and anger and feelings of rejection and self-pity to grow. This is directed not so much at your son anymore, but at yourself. Small wonder that by the end of the day you now think your son just can't be bothered with you, while in reality he is at least three day's walk from the nearest village and there's no cell phone coverage either.

If you are practicing giving out positive, healthy energy, then you should have all that you want and need and then some. You should also be balanced in yourself, be clearer and calmer in yourself. You should also know where you have come from, where you are now and where you are going to in the near future.

The power of the energy we have is more powerful than you might think. (Positive and negative energy are just as powerful as each other.) It is better to understand the huge responsibility we have been given, as with great power comes great responsibility. Give energy the respect it deserves and you will find you are rewarded. Not respecting the power of your energy is like not respecting the law. If you don't respect the law, you're likely to get into a lot of trouble which will cause even more worries and undue stress that you don't need. As with the law, give energy the respect it deserves and it will take good care of you for energy is life, energy is breath, and energy is your life force.

Who Is?

Who is your greatest Teacher and Guru? You are your greatest Teacher and your best student. You can learn so much from yourself and teach yourself so much.

So many go externally to find answers to questions they feel they cannot answer. Going externally as a first choice you give your energy and power away. If you are looking for an answer always start with yourself.

Do you feel a void in your life, be it that you are lonely, unhappy, bored and hungry and so on? The void is a lack of clarity within you. With *Who Stole My Energy* will give you knowledge that can assist you in helping you achieve success and assist you in ridding yourself of the void you may be feeling inside you now.

To remove the clutter from your mind and body, you remove clutter from your life and you can begin to see things a lot more clearly. Then with this new clarity you begin to see the answers for yourself, instead of going externally to get the answers. Each time you go externally for the answers, you give more and more of your power and energy away.

You are your greatest resource. You hold all the keys to the questions you have, like why can't I lose weight? Why can't I keep the weight off permanently? Why am I not successful in my life, be it in your relationships, business and/or financially? I am sure you have many more questions and that is wonderful because that means you still want to learn and grow. Many children learn at a fast rate because they ask questions, as adults we stop asking questions of ourselves and of life. If we take a lesson from children and continue to ask questions we will continue to grow and move forward in life. The more we move forward the more likely we are going to have opportunities coming into our lives. With each opportunity we have the option to grow and learn, and with each opportunity that comes into our life we have the opportunity to gain so much more.

Let's begin the path to clearing the clutter, by better understanding you. *Learning is not compulsory...neither is survival.*

- Francis Bacon

A famous storyteller came to a town, and a big group of people gathered around him. He had to shout his story so that everyone could hear. After the crowd had dissipated, he was still shouting. Someone asked why he was yelling when there was nobody there to listen. The sage said, "In the beginning I had to scream so that others could hear my story, but now I must scream so that I can hear the story." So often, we teach what we most need to learn. - The Zen Book. Daniel Levin

Throughout the pages of Who Stole My Energy you will read many quotes and sayings by myself and many others and each time you read them let them give you something new every time, allowing your mind and your spirit to grow, learn and evolve. You can also do this with the knowledge in Who Stole My Energy, how you read it today and how you read it another day will give you many different meanings and lessons. Allow your mind to open and expand and enjoy the journey into the self.

Circle of Energy

A loving person lives in a loving world.

A hostile person lives in a hostile world.

Everyone you meet is your mirror.

- Ken Keyes, Jr.

Handbook to Higher Consciousness.

Energy, like a circle, has no beginning and no end. Energy moves in circles around you and through you like a constant stream, putting out energy and getting it back.

Think of yourself; just a thought!

That is very powerful and that is energy you are putting out. Being aware of your thoughts for a day is truly a wonderful eye-opener. Start off by spending a day being aware of your thoughts. At the end of the day think back over all the thoughts you had, including all the ones you didn't even voice out loud. From the moment you wake up in the morning your thoughts are in full swing; you think this and that. But what are you really thinking? Is it constructive or destructive toward yourself or others?

If you are running late do you nurture yourself or run yourself down for over-sleeping or not being able to manage your time better? When you passed that mirror or shop window and saw your reflection did you think why did I wear this today? Or there may be room for improvement? This is all energy you are putting out and so the circle of energy begins its cycle out into the world and back around to you.

What you say about yourself in your own mind with your own thoughts is more powerful than you may realize, because with each thought you have sent out energy just as if you had spoken the words from your very lips. The rule is; what went out must come back as part of the constant circle of energy. Such negativity might come back in the form of gossiping, people lying to you, people hurting you, or – just to give you an idea – it may even come back as abuse! If you are aware of your thoughts you can stop negative energy going out and so stop such negative energy coming into your life.

So how do you look at yourself running late? First, be a little more nurturing, and remember it is a choice you have made. If you are late for an appointment you chose to be late, because if you wanted to be on time you would have left earlier and been on time. You may think that is too black and white, but I will admit, that I believe in a black and white world; there is no gray area. Gray areas are created for people to hide in so they have a wonderful excuse and won't have to deal with something. Many people hide in the gray area for the rest of their lives. That is their choice. But to live in a gray area in a black and white world leaves everyone else in control of your life. It means that you choose to put parts, if not all of your life in the 'too hard box'.

Just imagine the energy you put out when you decide to use the gray area, and the energy that comes back.

If your output is unclear, blurred and cloudy because it comes through your gray area, then that is the energy that will come back to you or that you will draw into your life; unclear, blurred and cloudy. When you live in a black and white world you draw in more clarity, people are more straightforward and clear instead of beating around the bush or taking forever to ask for something.

We are so unaware of what we are doing, thinking and saying sometimes. Let's be honest; for some of us it is most times. Most people say, 'Hello, how are you?' and then just keep walking. I like to reply with a cheeky; 'Do you really want to know or are you just being polite?' I have had some interesting responses.

When you use your thoughts to judge yourself in a negative way you draw in negative energy. The negative judgments you have about yourself in thought or word or action will be returned to you, for example in the form of people not treating you very nicely. For example, you could walk into a shop you have never been into and be treated rudely by a staff member. You blame that person for being rude. When you go externally to fix an energy problem like this you give your power away; you give your energy away. Blame something or someone and you lose power, energy, and so you begin to lose more control over your own life.

If someone is rude to you, in most cases they are reacting to the energy you put out or to energy that infects (see the next section on Infecting Energy). Stop for a moment and take back your control, your power and say why did this happen? Understand why it happened. Did you put out negative energy? Taking responsibility for everything that happens to you is taking back your control and your power. Next time someone is rude to you, go internally to fix the energy problem. Going external, you lose power and control of your life. You choose to give your power away or not. Which is healthier for you?

Judging another with a thought or word is actually one of your greatest teachers. When you judge another you are still putting out energy and it will be returned. When you judge another, it is merely a reflection of how you feel about yourself. If you run someone down, that is actually how you feel about yourself. If you praise another person, that too is how you feel about yourself. For example, a fitness fanatic says he doesn't like it when people don't take pride in their bodies, and let themselves go. This judgment shows me that even though he is good looking, he is still very insecure about himself and the way he looks to others. It is very sad and I feel for him. When I see someone out of shape I look at them and I think they are either in a lot of pain, or they are resisting change in their lives, resisting moving forward in some area of their life. I try to understand all that I see and experience and I find that when I do, it always leads to feelings of compassion for others.

The actions of men are the best interpreters

of their thoughts. —John Locke

If you hear a person talking about you and judging you, that is how they feel about themselves. It is also an indication of the sort of energy they put out and get back. If someone says something unpleasant about you, realize they cannot say that unless they feel on some level much the same about themselves. Next time someone puts you down you will realize that this is how he or she feel about themselves and with this understanding will come compassion. The put-down loses its power over you and you take back control.

If you find it still bothers you or has triggered you, then you may have been giving out a negative energy either in putting yourself down or another, so take responsibility for this experience and take back your power.

The energy we put out every day comes back and shows not only us, but also the world how we feel about ourselves and the kind of person we are. It shows the kind of energy we are putting out and whether we are healthy or unhealthy.

When you understand energy you understand there are no secrets. All that you are and all that you think you are hiding is really displayed openly for everyone to see. Knowing this you may want to be more aware of your energy and the energy of others. It is all a matter of watching the energy you are putting out with each thought, feeling, action and word.

Infecting Energy

Keep company with the wise

and you will become wise.

If you make friends with stupid people,

you will be ruined.

The Good News Bible, Proverbs:

Chapter 13, Verse 20.

We have a responsibility to ourselves to be selective about who we spend time with. If you spent a lot of time with someone who, for instance, likes running people down, you will find you will begin to do the same. Why? Because the energy of another can infect you, for a day, a week, or even longer.

If you wanted to give up smoking for your loved ones, your health and for financial reasons, then you wouldn't spend time with smokers. You may think it is just the temptation of being around other smokers that will weaken you. It isn't. It is their energy infecting you. If you do spend time with smokers you are setting yourself up to fail. You must move out of your comfort zone, which has given you a sense of security so far. The comfort zone has an invisible force you have to push against to get yourself free of smoking. Being around other people who enjoy smoking, who associate smoking with that cup of coffee, associate smoking with food or social situations, you will be infected by that energy. You know that energy very well and it will make it very easy for you to fall back into the smoking habit; back into your comfort zone.

When you are ready and feel you have achieved your goal, you may be able to spend time with the people you know who smoke. But spending time with them, their energy will infect you and you may still find you want that cigarette again. It is your choice to smoke a cigarette or not to smoke a cigarette. You choose to buy a pack of cigarettes, just like you choose to be infected by the energy of others who smoke cigarettes. It is always your choice and no one else's. If you have succeeded in giving up and really understood and realized the power and control you have over your own energy now and be aware of it, then you are going to be stronger and more able to succeed in shielding yourself from the energy emanating from people who smoke.

Quitting smoking is the easiest thing in the world.

I've done it hundreds of times.

-Mark Twain.

Energy is very powerful. It can change you in just a short time. How many times have you walked into a room where someone has just had an argument and literally felt the discomfort in the room? That is energy you are feeling, and that is effecting you.

If you spend time with someone who is very angry all the time you too will become angry. How does that work? The person's energy infects you and you react. You probably have suppressed anger from a past experience that you have not dealt with and the person who infected you with their angry energy triggers you into a reaction.

If you go externally and react to being infected with angry energy you just add more problems to what you have already suppressed. The anger then remains within you, ready to resurface again. But if you go internally and try to understand why you are angry, then you take the opportunity to heal yourself and the situation. You will find you are able to clear the anger and return to your calm state of mind.

To go internally, first remove yourself from the room for a moment. If need be, go to the bathroom, but remove yourself from the energy that is infecting you. Ask yourself what you are feeling right now. Are you feeling irritated, frustrated, annoyed? Then once you are aware of what it is, realize that these emotional responses are coming from suppressed feelings from past situations. It may be, for example, that you are irritated over something you just did that day that it has not been cleared; it could be an energy block (see next section on Energy Blocks).

Once you are aware of what has surfaced in you, see if you can clear it. If you can't seem to clear it, then take the time to write down everything that you are feeling if possible and you will come to your own clarity. I have found by writing everything out, you become clearer a lot faster than if you try to just work it out in your head, which can cause the frustration and irritation to grow as you go round in circles in your own mind. You can get stuck on one part of the solution and not see the bigger picture. By writing it all down you will find that it all begins to unravel. It is not difficult to take back your control and power. It is a choice that makes life a little lighter, a little clearer.

By writing down what is going on for you, and writing down your feelings, and your emotions that may surface you begin to see them more clearly, you begin to understand yourself more, and become aware of what is blocking you from moving forward in what you want to achieve in life, or blocking you from having the life you want.

Take for example, you are meant to be exercising daily, you promised yourself this, and you miss a workout maybe even two workouts. Without realizing it you are more upset at yourself then you want to admit at the time, as you have to or want to get on with your day. You get on with your day, but you start being very hard on yourself about everything that comes up through out the day, you might even feel frustrated or angry. If you write your feelings down you will be able to see where it stems from, and once you know the source then it clears its self, so you stop being hard on yourself; that frustration and anger disappears and you feel so much better in yourself.

Not long ago I spoke to a woman who said that she longed so much to meditate, yet she couldn't calm her mind. I said, "Fine. Instead of calming your mind, just watch it. As your thoughts wander, wander with them. Watch them go from place to place and see what happens." Several days later she told me that as soon as she stopped trying to control her mind, it stopped battling her and just relaxed on its own.

Funny how that works, isn't it?

—Daniel Levin, *The Zen Book.*

What if you are a happy person and you spend time with an angry person? Why can't the happiness you feel infect the angry person? Because you have suppressed anger; you don't have suppressed happiness. We take full responsibility for being happy which means staying in our own power and control. But when we are angry we often find an external source to blame, thereby giving our power and control away and suppressing the emotion.

It is important that you make yourself aware of incidences when another person's negativity may be infecting you. But on the bonus side another person's energy that is infecting you is an opportunity to learn, to be more aware and to use the opportunity to make changes in your life for the better.

Remember that energy only takes a moment to infect you but it can become your own permanent energy, and remain with you for months, years or even for the rest of your life if you choose. For example if you spent much time with people who have no desire to move forward in life, who like to resist and block every opportunity, you will become infected with this energy. Such energy can really become part of you and affect you the same way becoming something you have to actively work to clear and overcome.

Most energy that infects will permeate the body to your very soul, and so you must work through it to clear that energy. The solution is to realize that such negative energy has infected you and to stay aware of this, stay alert and aware that this is your life, your health and your future and it can be a good future or it can be something else.

Staying aware is at first a task and a chore but after time you won't even think about it and then you will watch life change.

If you are aware of being infected by energy, the emotions you feel will be recognized straight away. Then you won't have to feed into the emotion or the energy that has just infected you. Instead of becoming overwhelmed by an emotion, you can feel the emotion then realize the emotion has a job; it's sending you a signal. Then you can take an opportunity to learn from this lesson and from all life's lessons and elevate and what I mean by elevate is to grow, also to elevate is to develop, grow spiritually and personally. If you elevate, others will elevate around you as you infect them with your personal energy.

Energy Blocks

Whatever is flexible and flowing will tend to grow,

whatever is rigid and blocked will wither and die.

—Tao Te Ching

Earlier I mentioned energy blocks, and the best way to define them is to explain how they are created in the first place.

Creating an energy block is very simple – just ignore your feelings and emotions. To explain the impact, imagine that your emotions and feelings are like an alarm clock. The alarm clock sounds and beeps and beeps and shocks you back into reality from your slumber, waking you up. You normally, of course, turn the annoying beeping alarm off as it's done its job. But imagine if you didn't. Imagine that you leave the beeping alarm on and it follows you around all day. The beeping alarm clock has done its job, but because you didn't deal with it, it has now become a major irritation.

Your emotions, like the alarm clock, have a job to do. But many people do not realize this and so they let that emotion run all day – way past the useful stage. If you, for instance, get angry at someone and then instead of being able to deal with the anger and/or incidence you have to attend to something else like a meeting. You can't walk into this important meeting feeling angry so you put on a brave face and store the anger. Most times it is then forgotten about, but the stored or suppressed anger and/or emotion has become an energy block. It becomes an energy block because you did not let the emotion do its job.

The job of an emotion is to teach. Wisdom masquerades as emotions and feelings. When an emotion surfaces it is an opportunity to recognize another lesson. Once the lesson is achieved you can move forward in life a lot quicker than if you suppress the emotion and allow it to become an energy block.

What happens to the suppressed energy block? Remember, energy is always moving, either forward in a constructive way, or backwards in a destructive way.

When you suppress the emotion and create the block, the energy is no longer flowing as it should naturally do. It is trapped; blocked into a confined space. The energy starts to become destructive because it has not been allowed to move through its natural process. Energy blocks create pain and health problems of all kinds, clouding your mind and depleting useful energy. They make life a little uncomfortable at least, creating pitfalls and ruts that may seem difficult to get out of. With a number of them, they can make life seem like a very dark tunnel in which there doesn't seem to be a light at the end.

The energy block is like having a hole in your petrol tank. You are losing precious energy every moment of every day. Where does the energy go that you are losing? Remember that when you get angry with someone you are sending him or her energy. Even your energy block has created negative energy which emanates from you. Whoever you focus on, be it in a good way or a bad way, receives your energy. That suppressed anger that you did not deal with is still sending energy to that person. That is where the energy has gone.

How do you remove energy blocks? You might choose to clear it yourself, through carefully reflecting, or better, writing down exactly how you are feeling about each emotion; and be honest or it won't work. Realize that anger is fear based, so when you get angry, for instance, you are actually triggered by something you are afraid of. (See Chapter 2 on Emotional Behaviour for a fuller explanation about emotions and what emotions are teaching us. If you understand the job of emotions you can clear the energy blocks created by them.)

Alternatively, you can talk to a close friend, a therapist or a spiritual counselor about how you are feeling and clear blocks this way. Sometimes, without realizing it, people find their energy blocks are stirred up and come to the surface when they see a massage therapist, an acupuncturist, a chiropractor, osteopath, homeopath and so on. They may shift energy blocks, which once they come up must be dealt with to clear them.

With time, your awareness of your emotions and feelings will grow with each moment of each day and as a result it will become second nature to you. As you start to be more aware of your emotions and feelings every day it will get a little easier to identify emotions as they arise making it easier to deal with them. This new habit of awareness becomes just like brushing your teeth or even breathing; you don't think about it, you just do it.

If you are truly aware of your emotions and feelings, you learn and grow from these opportunities and few energy blocks accumulate inside of you. Life becomes a little easier and a lot clearer, you'll feel more energetic and even your health can and will improve.

Everyone has energy blocks. If you didn't, you wouldn't be human. The thing is to keep your energy blocks to a minimum level at which you can cope a lot better, then maintain this state through awareness and understanding. Realize that your emotions and feelings are tools to make life a little easier. Understand that each emotion and feeling is a life tool that is trying to show you and teach you something.

This is a different way of looking at your emotions and feelings. You now have a new understanding. What you do with this new knowledge is up to you. If you have been a slave to your emotions and feelings, why not take back your power and control and empower your life?

Giving Your Energy Away

We stumble and fall constantly even when we are most enlightened. But when we are in true spiritual darkness, we do not even know that we have fallen.

-David Baird. *a Thousand Paths to wisdom*

We are constantly giving our energy away. As soon as we focus on something or someone we give our energy away without even realizing it. You realize now though! If you focus on anything, you are giving your energy, giving your life force away.

Let me use anger again, as an example of giving energy away as it is one energy draining emotion that many people are familiar with. When you are angry or upset at someone you are giving away large amounts of your energy. It is flowing out of you at a rapid speed. You may not be consciously aware of this, but sub-consciously you will feel a drop in your energy levels.

As the anger grows stronger and stronger; you become more irritable and even more annoyed at the person you are angry at. You think it is because you are so angry, and it may have started as that. But you have given away so much energy that you are resenting the other person. You need to find a way to get your energy back or get your energy, life force levels back up.

Then comes the intimidation, where you may stand over someone physically smaller than you to get your energy back. Because as soon as you put fear into them, the energy starts to be returned to you and you feel powerful again. People can intimidate in different ways with their many strengths beyond physical alone, including intellect, maturity, social position or spiritual power. Through such strengths you know you will intimidate another person – not necessarily the same person who made you angry in the first place – and get your energy back.

Intimidation can result in different forms of abuse from physical to emotional e.g. the silent intimidator, who gives you the silent treatment. They stop talking and ignore you which can be just as abusive as someone who is verbally abusive, and the result for them is the same; his or her energy levels go up.

Having this new knowledge and awareness, and coming across situations where you see intimidators at work, you will understand what is going on, and the whole situation if you are aware will de-escalate. Situations that may have triggered you when someone intimidated you before, will lose their power over you. You will see straight through them and understand exactly what they are doing. With this new awareness and understanding you have again taken back your power.

You make a choice about getting angry with someone. You make a choice to give your energy away and you make a choice to become an intimidator to get your energy levels back up. What else do you do to give your energy away? Who do you intimidate to get energy back?

Your subconscious knows that if you lose your life force, your energy, you will cease to exist. When you give your energy away there is a mad rush, anxiety, panic that develops and drives you to get that energy back. How can you stop this vicious circle repeating itself? Be more aware of when and how you are giving too much energy away and stop it. Life was never meant to be hard. People make it that way.

It is okay to be angry, it is an emotion and remember each emotion has a job to do. But don't get stuck in the emotion because then it is no longer doing its job. Stop feeding into your emotions and start letting your emotions do their job. Acknowledge your anger or emotion and remembering again that anger is fear-based, note that you must be afraid of something or something has made you feel vulnerable. Stop and ask yourself what it is that you fear. No one else needs to know the answer – just you. Let the anger-emotion do its job and you will find anger can be a very healthy and helpful emotion. But if you feed the emotion of anger, you will begin the vicious cycle and the predator and prey behaviors' repeat endlessly. This is your choice.

You have the control and power over your own life. Decide wisely, because all energy you put out, as a rule will come back. There is no cancelling out energy. What you have just put out; you have to live with. Be aware you need to keep your eye on the ball at all times to make sure you are getting exactly what you want, and are asking for. Make energy work for you, not against you.

Making Energy Work for You

If you have built castles in the air, your work need not be lost. Now put foundations under them.

-Osa Johnson

How do you make energy work for you? We learn at a young age, how to get energy. For example, take a young child that goes to its mother or father to show them a picture they drew. The parent is cooking dinner or on the telephone, or maybe having a cup of coffee with friends, when the child goes over and shows them the drawing. The parent says, 'That's nice dear,' and puts it aside, then sends the child away. The child only receives a little of the parent's attention and energy.

The child then breaks something by accident. The mother or father rushes into the room and yells at the child, annoyed, angry and very upset. The child may not understand at such a young age but the child feels a lift inside. Full attention feels good. The child may not consciously know what they are feeling but subconsciously they will know their life force just increased and it felt good. This memory is then stored in the sub-conscious of the child.

The parent may continue to be upset for a long time after, which means the child continues to receive energy. If the child is good they get a small amount of energy, and if they are naughty they get much more energy. From situations like this, from our first guru, our first teacher, our mother or father, we learn how to make energy work for us; how to get energy. Sometimes this is not a healthy way to get energy but we discover what works and if continuing to be demanding and destructive is the best prospect, it is most likely to be chosen.

But remember, that putting out negative, destructive energy, brings hardships with it ...

The energy we put out is so important: it can be very constructive, healing, helpful and bring so much success, happiness and even love. So why do so many of us choose to put out negative, destructive energy instead of the more positive, constructive and helpful energy?

Take responsibility for everything that happens to you and for what is not happening to you and you take back your power and control over your life, instead of having energy control you. Nothing can happen to you without you first putting the energy out there to draw it in. The secret of making your energy work for you is to be aware of your own energy and what other energies are infecting you from other people. Once you are aware that a negative energy has infected you or come to the fore, then you can clear this energy.

Know that there is no Karma: there are only lessons and you are the one responsible for drawing the lessons in. There is no 'good luck' and there is no 'bad luck' only what you yourself create with your own energy. Understanding this is your key to freedom, your key to taking back your power and your control over your life.

You may have felt like your power and control have been taken from you at certain stages in your life, but no one can take anything from you unless you put out the energy and draw the situations or experiences into your life that made you feel powerless. Take back that power by understanding the energy you put out. Be it good energy or bad energy, it will draw in the good or bad; you are in control of your life. Take back your power, your control and your choice.

Making energy work for you can be used to get what you really want in life. Just be sure that what you decide to seek is what you truly want and that you are not being infected by anyone else's energy. Infected by energy of another person you could start wanting what they want, until you actually receive it – and then realization dawns and you turn around and ask yourself why you wanted it. If you realize energy infects, you can see where any desire actually came from, making you more aware in the future of what it is you truly want. Once you are back in control of your power, let's see how you might use that power in your life. For example, a question I get asked time and time again is how to draw someone into one's life; a relationship or a soul mate. First, look at the energy you put out. Are you judging yourself or others in a negative way? Are you constantly complaining? Are you forever anxious about meeting someone, and demanding why aren't they in my life right now? Are you upset at life and believe life is being unfair because you have no one in your life at this moment? Do you constantly whine and say, 'Why me? This isn't fair. All my other friends are getting married and I am getting left on the shelf!'(just a few examples of what I have seen people say and do). This becomes the energy that they are putting out. Who in their right mind would be attracted to that; a person who is demanding, complaining, whining, negative, judgmental – and not in a constructive way, highly strung or anxious? You get the picture.

If you managed to attract someone into your life while putting out that sort of energy, what kind of person is he or she likely to be? For example, if you spend time with a friend who is having an affair with someone who is married then you are going to draw that energy into your life. As a result, the energy infecting you may result in you being drawn to having an affair, or a partner you draw in won't be the honest, faithful kind you may be hoping for. But do remember the energy we put out does not always come back to us in the same package, but it will be returned to you.

Most people believe they want a nurturing, loving, supportive relationship so the question they need to ask themselves is 'Is that the energy I'm putting out?' Stop and look at what energy you are putting out. Then look at the energy you live in at home, the energy that is surrounding you and infecting you; this all comes into the equation. Once you have made yourself aware of the energy you are putting out, ask yourself, would you be attracted to that? Now be honest. Okay be real honest. No, I said be honest!

The reason I say be 'honest' is because when I ask 'Would you be attracted to that?' the first answer I get in most cases is 'Yes!'. Once people get honest with themselves, however, they say 'Well ... no!'. If they are honest from the start it makes the job a lot easier. The solution is simple. Change the energy you are putting out to draw in the relationship you want.

Judge yourself in a negative way with your thoughts, words or actions and you draw in someone who will lie to you and/or abuse you on some level. Take responsibility for the energy you put out and you will draw in what you really want and need.

Judge yourself in a positive way with your thoughts, words and actions and you are sure to draw in a much healthier relationship. I know it may be difficult to give up on judging yourself in a negative way because so many of us have done it for so long. It is a learnt behavior and you are undoing years of programming. But if you at least improve on it, you improve your chances of drawing that special someone into your life.

Being aware of what sort of energy you are putting out and realizing the power you have to draw to you what you need just isn't about relationships. You can make energy really work for you and as a result grow into a happier, healthier person.

Energy Summary

*If you can understand just one thing thoroughly,
then you will understand everything.*

—David Baird, a Thousands Paths to wisdom.

With each chapter in *Who Stole My Energy?* you will become a little more knowledgeable, aware and empowered to grow by your personal understanding.

Energy is part of us (our life force) and understanding how energy works offers a great way to have insights into the interactions and reactions of yourself and others around you. The relationship of being both predator and prey for energy can make getting energy a constant battle. Understanding the relationship you have with energy lets you stop being energy prey for others to feed off. Being aware also stops you being a predator taking energy from others and filling up yourself with temporary or negative energy that only serves to make you feel good or powerful for a short while. Understanding energy and having control over it, allows you to build up your levels of positive energy and gives you more clarity to find your direction in life.

Life is a mirror, it reflects your secrets and your soul. Energy reflects you always, every moment of every day. You can never hide from energy, as it is always reflecting back to you who you truly are being and what you really are asking for. You don't need to seek answers from others because they are reflected back to you in your thoughts, words and everyday situations and conversations. If you are honest with yourself, you will realize you hold all the answers to all of your personal questions about life.

Lessons we learn today can change our lives forever. I hope that learning this little about energy will change your life for the better and give you insights into yourself and others.

If I may share something with you that a very good friend of mine emailed to me after reading this section on energy. I was so touched and moved at how she captured what I was trying to say that I knew I had to share this. I hope you find it insightful.

> *Who Stole My Energy?* is about each person as an individual and what and how they deal with things in their own lives. It teaches the individual to try to cope with their actions and be responsible for themselves, but most of all, to know that they have the power within to change their own destiny.

> Life is a matter of choice as to how we react to each and every situation. What I have come to learn is that when I am a lot calmer about things I am able to cope and deal with things in a more pleasant way/manner.

> *—Elizabeth Cuthers*

> *Brisbane, Australia.*

Chapter 2   Emotional Behaviour

Your joy is your own;

Your bitterness is your own.

No one can share them with you.

—The Good News Bible, Proverbs:

Chapter 14, Verse 10

Emotions have a job to do like every other part of you does. Your emotions are just as much a part of you as your eyes, ears, hands, feet or internal organs. Every part of you has a job and this includes your emotions and everything that you feel.

When someone gets a job promotion, they feel the excitement, they own the whole experience and take credit for the promotion – and so they should. But when they lose their job and feel the associated emotions, they may disown the whole experience and wonder how this happened to them. Everything we feel and experience in life is every bit a part of us. To disown a feeling or an experience that we created is sending out the wrong kind of energy, and do you really want that returned to you?

Many people like to store their emotions and feelings away in a closet; like skeletons. Telling people how we really feel is sometimes like sharing a big secret. These secrets build up and the closet gets pretty crowded. The closet door starts to bulge and soon cracks begin to show as the burden becomes unbearably heavy. You have been living a lie by storing so many skeletons. It is very exhausting to keep up just one lie, but imagine accumulating many lies that you live with and have built up over many years. Many people live like this every day of their lives.

As a result of living a life with secrets, skeletons in the closet and keeping up lies, we become drained, tired, exhausted. We start to suffer from emotional pain which always leads to physical discomfort or pain, illness and dis-ease. It can also stop you from having the life you truly want and/or deserve.

Once the burden becomes so heavy that you struggle to find your way, it is like being lost in the darkness. You may lose sight of your personal life path and wonder where to go next in your life, career, relationship search for a healthier you.

Let's learn to understand our emotions and become aware of their real purpose. Then you may not be so ashamed to show emotions, or afraid to show how you are truly feeling. When you begin to see your emotions as a tool to be used to help navigate your way through this life, you are not only taking back your power but you are learning to trust yourself. The more you trust yourself, the more chance you have of making your way back to your true inner-self. When you trust yourself and believe in yourself and what you are saying, you will find, more and more, that things that once bothered you won't bother you anymore, making life's road a little less difficult to travel.

Give your power away to your emotions and you will watch things around you unravel. This is not fate being unkind, or everything being your fault that things are going wrong. It is you feeding into your emotions. Life only seems to unravel, it is really you giving your power away and when you do give away your power you lose balance.

If you entered a new job in which you didn't know what you were doing, it would give you a great deal of emotional stress. Your anxiety levels would be pretty high. Why? Because you are working in the dark. That is pretty much where most people are with their emotions much of the time – in the dark. In the following sections in this chapter, I am going to help you understand your own emotions and their real purpose and bring you into the daylight.

Understanding

Emotions are not fleeting events isolated in mental space; they are expressions of awareness, the fundamental stuff of life.

-Deepak Chopra, M.D. Ageless Body, Timeless Mind.
A Companion Guide and Journal.

You may think that the word understanding is of those over-used words that should be deleted from our dictionaries and it may even trigger a response in you where you say "Ho-hum, yawn" or it may make you feel like stamping your feet and yelling "If someone says I have to be understanding one more time, you truly feel you could not bear it one more time." You will come across the word many times in these chapters and I make no apologies for it. Understanding is a great way to help you deal with your emotions and feelings and life in general. Using understanding as a daily tool is going to help you lighten that load you are burdened with. All understanding leads to having compassion and to a healthier you. Understanding is about awareness and therefore having the tools to gain more insights and better read yourself and others both very healing. This chapter is about understanding your emotions and being aware of them.

Understanding leads to a calmer you; it helps you to better understand people, situations, emotions, feelings and anything in general.

If your partner, child or friend were to foolishly break an item that you really value, would you yell and scream at them? Would you then spend the next week or so walking around on eggshells and not being able to look them in the eye? Once an item is broken you can't change that fact. It is broken! But you can understand the situation more.

What if you were to say, 'It is broken, and you realize you did wrong and that's it; why lose sleep over something that has happened that we can't change?' You will have a little more calm in your life. And believe me the person who broke the item will be so surprised that you may even have to convince them it is okay, really. That person who broke the item will have learnt a great deal more as a result of your one small action than if you had yelled and screamed.

Imagine you walk into a shop to pay for an item you have ordered and the item is not the correct one or has changed upwards in price. You can jump up and down, yell at the shop assistant and generally give your energy away, making the shop assistant's day worse than it already may have been so that pretty much doesn't help anyone and so no one really wins in the end. However you do get to take the item home. Each time thereafter that you look at that item you will think about that shop assistant – and guess where your energy will go. You might think, 'Well I have my correct item at the correct price, so I won!' but the energy you have attached to the item is going to always send your personal energy to the shop assistant. With a little understanding of the situation you could have made other choices, such as either just paying the price or leaving it; the lesson being that with understanding, your life is a little calmer and a lot healthier for you.

Getting needlessly upset, makes for an uncomfortable environment for a long time after and who wants that? The calm approach saves so much time and saves you undoing damage you may cause to a friendship or relationship. Also from understanding such situations you save putting out a negative energy that must come back. So being understanding can also be a time saver and makes life a bit more bearable.

Understanding can help when you hear family or friends putting someone down. It may annoy you, as you don't want to be dragged into a negative conversation. But with a little understanding the conversation will lose its power. Understand that when one person judges another, be it in a positive way or a negative way, that is how they truly feel about themselves. So next time you hear a conversation where someone is putting someone down, then remember that what they are criticizing is only how they feel about themselves.

If you ask someone, 'What do you honestly think of me?' they will tell you, and you may be surprised at what you hear. You may even think they left so much out because you see yourself as more confident and outgoing perhaps, and they didn't see that. Why? Because they can only see what is in themselves; in their very souls.

Many people lead by example, on a daily basis, without even realizing it. Most would not realize the impact they have on the lives of others without ever meaning to or seeking to lead. So where are you going when you lead others? Where are you leading these people? With a little understanding you may be able to lead others as well as yourself to a better life. We can help others, because we infect them with our energy when we talk to them on the telephone or spend time in their company. So you can infect others with an energy that is healthy and positive, and so helping others in this way. Understand this and be responsible for yourself. You have a great impact on the people you care about and the people you come in contact with.

When you do badly by others because you don't understand a situation, you have not sinned, but when you do understand a situation and you do it anyway, you have sinned. Maybe that is why we have avoided understanding for so long. Saying, 'Yes, I understand,' is one thing. Living out that understanding is quite another because true understanding may be difficult to follow up on at first, and you may even be initially reluctant to work through it. But it will always lead you to compassion and to a calmer and healthier you.

If you take the time to understand, truly understand yourself, everything else you need in your life will be drawn to you. You won't want for anything because everything you may have wanted once will be drawn to you. So how can you want for something you already have? Understanding you will get you a lot closer to knowing your true self and trusting your true inner self. Start with taking some time to understand you first and you will become a magnet for what you need and want.

Awareness

Understanding Awareness is so very helpful. Why? If you put awareness into practice then you begin to be able to become more sensitive to your surroundings and to everything and everyone in your life be it in your personal or professional life.

I always ask people to start with themselves first when it comes to beginning practicing the understanding of awareness. In fact some people only focus their awareness on themselves as it is a real eye opener.

First, start with being aware of yourself, be aware of your fleeting-thoughts, day-dreams, what you say, your actions, your feelings and emotions, your tone of voice, your facial expressions, your body language, how you react when you see someone or something. Be aware of your surroundings that affect you.

By starting with yourself you begin to see life through a very different set of glasses. Everyday spend time being aware of yourself on as many levels as you can dream up.

First be aware of yourself; then ask yourself if someone looked at me like that, or spoke to me like that, or treated me like that would I like it? If the answer is 'no' then if you like, ask yourself why are you treating yourself like that?

From first being aware of yourself gives you a clear view of how you are treating other people. As if you treat yourself poorly or your thoughts are negative judgements of others then it gives you amazing insights into how you treat others even if you are not fully aware. Don't be surprised that you are not fully aware of how you treat yourself or how negative your feelings, emotions, thoughts, actions and more maybe. I find most people are walking around completely asleep and they like it that way, if it isn't broken don't fix it, right? The other one you may have heard is 'it is better the devil you know then the devil you don't', one way of seeing it is, why rock the boat.

Here is the reward that comes with understanding awareness and practicing awareness. Is the more you are awake or aware the more sensitive you become to everything and everyone around you. Have you ever been interested in profiling or another name for it is 'reading people'? If the answer is 'yes' then practicing awareness daily is a great place to start, it may look like it could be boring but it soon becomes like a walk in the part.

The only warning I have for anyone who is interested in practicing being more aware is that once you turn it on it is difficult to turn off and for some impossible.

Once you are aware of yourself this awareness begins to filter into other parts of your life and you begin to read people in your home and personal life and workplace and professional life.

After you become aware of yourself, you naturally start to become aware of other people in your life, even in social situations. If you know the person, you might like to ask them if you could share something personal you picked up about them, it could help them. Do remember when you talk to someone or share with another, ask yourself would you like it if anyone talked to you like that?

All that is shared within these pages of this book are insights and different points of view that will give you other ways to practice awareness.

Who Stole My Energy? is a book to get you started, building blocks to awareness of self and then of others.

Remember I can only show you the door you have to walk through it. Also in this first book these are my beliefs for you to see through a different set of glasses, or a different viewpoint it is now up to you to create your very own beliefs and these new beliefs of your own will come about through the help of practicing daily the understand of awareness.

I can only wish you well on your journey to discovery through Awareness and Understanding and through the insights shared within these pages of Who Stole My Energy?

Understanding Anger

A gentle answer quiets anger,

but a harsh one stirs it up.

—The Good News Bible, Proverbs:

Chapter 15, Verse 1

Anger is an emotion that has been used to illustrate my point a number of times already. I have been talking about it so far as if we all understand exactly what anger is, though we don't really, so let's clear it up and give you the clear-cut version of what anger really is. Anger is a very old response to fear. When faced with something scary, we can choose to run or stay and face it – flight or fight. If you choose to stay your body provides you with the chemicals, like adrenaline, to best prepare you for that. It is these chemicals that give you that hot, wide-awake, ready-to-hit something feeling we associate with feeling angry.

But in our society today, such an extreme response to staying and facing up to something scary is often not necessary. We need to put our body at rest again or these chemicals keep being pumped in, and if that happens too often, they do harm to your health.

So we must recognize that the feeling of anger is just an emotion; an expression of something we are feeling, a signal asking us to respond. The anger we are feeling has a job to do like everything else that is a part of us, but then it should be sent on its way. If we feed into our anger and get really upset, we aren't really allowing the anger to do its job. We are also giving our energy away to whatever or whoever triggered the anger in the first place – yes you can even give an actual object like your troublesome car or your faulty television set your energy, because everything is the same energy. We should feel our emotions, because it is very healthy to do so, but people feel the emotion for minutes, which turn into hours and so on. Then nothing actually gets accomplished. When you feel the anger, acknowledge that you are feeling angry and take the time to be aware that you are angry. Then, remind yourself that anger is fear-based and ask yourself what it is that you are afraid of or what has made you feel vulnerable.

Most times when people are angry, something or someone has taken them out of their comfort zone. A change has been presented to them and most people are afraid of change. They have been pushed to move forward in life – maybe only in a small way, maybe a huge move forward – and fear arises. People don't like to accept that they are feeling afraid because it makes them feel vulnerable so they hold on to an emotion, such as anger, that has made them feel powerful in the past. This of course is a behaviour learnt from those around them when they were growing up.

Anger fills their body and so they suppress their fear. They can't clear the anger because it is actually fear-based. They need to face their fear that is suppressed to move forward and so an energy block is created from this suppressed feeling.

I mentioned earlier how if you walk into a room where someone has just had an argument, you can feel the energy in the room. You know that someone has just had an argument and got pretty angry. Like most other people you won't stay very long or will back out of the room, because anger is a very strong emotion and our faithful subconscious that stores every situation and experience in our life, soon tells us that if we remain in that situation it may not be safe. Energy levels at least will be affected, even if the physical self is safe and people subconsciously know this. Your energy would turn to the two people who were just arguing as soon as you focus on them. And if you are drawn into the argument a battle for energy will begin quite possibly leaving you drained. No one walks into a room of happy people and wants to get out of there, because happy people most of the time aren't going to do battle with you to get energy.

Anger of course can lead to verbal, emotional, and mental abuse and can escalate to physical abuse, affecting most people for a very long time – maybe for the rest of their lives. After someone is abused, they will usually begin to suppress anger themselves.

When you first become angry you lose energy to the person who triggered you. Know that when you feed anger and allow yourself to remain angry, a battle starts for energy. You feel an urgent need to get back the energy you are losing to anger. The urgency to get the energy back grows. You panic. You become very anxious and you find ways to get the energy back in a hurry; your life is actually at stake. You may not be consciously aware of how fatal it is but your subconscious knows the urgency. What would you do to save your own life?

It is at this point that someone becomes an intimidator and in bad cases, in the worst cases, even abusive. They take back their energy with force. All they know is it feels good and so they keep doing it. They then pass the behaviour onto their children and the pattern continues. The abuse may not be physical but there are other ways to abuse someone. Do remember it is a choice; we all still have a choice. But because of the lack of understanding of anger and what is happening the abuser may not see and takes back their energy the only way they know how. This does not make it right, but this is a fact of so many people's lives.

Not every anger situation is given the attention it deserves. When you become angry or someone close to you does, try to understand the situation, and if you can, try to understand the causes of the anger. Then everyone wins. (If it's your own outburst of anger ask yourself what has made you feel vulnerable or afraid, or if it's someone else's you can ask them what is making them feel vulnerable.) You are giving out an understanding energy, one of compassion, generosity and caring for someone else's well being. This is the energy you will draw into your life. When the energy comes back it may not be packaged the way you sent it out, but it will come back in a positive way.

Anger is a wonderful teacher, and holds many lessons. Lessons and experiences that lead to knowledge and knowledge leads to great wisdom.

The emotion of anger has a job and its job is to give us a signal that we are afraid; to show us that we need to understand why we are afraid and to clear away the cause. Clear the anger instead of feeding into the emotion or you will lose sight of what prompted it in the first place and you will lose sight of the lessons and an opportunity to elevate and grow yourself.

Understanding Fear

Before we can make friends with anyone else, we must first make friends with ourselves.

-Eleanor Roosevelt.

Fear is another feeling, another emotion and another great teacher. Fear is also a great protector. Fear is a tool of survival. The job of fear is actually to keep us safe from harm.

Fear stops us from taking a walk on the highway in peak hour traffic. Fear stops us from running around on the ledge of a very tall building. Fear stops us from taking long walks on our own through a park in the middle of the night. Fear is a wonderful guardian.

But fear can also be used as a cage; as an easy way out of trying anything new that we are looking for an excuse to avoid. Ask someone why they don't want to do something and they will often say they are afraid.

Ask that person to remove the word 'Fear' from their vocabulary and say, 'Now why can't you do it?' Here you may actually get to the truth of the matter and find out what is really going on.

Couples in relationships become afraid sometimes but they don't even realize it. They start to fight and argue over every little thing, avoiding the one thing they need to talk about, the bigger something, the elephant standing in the room. Many people, male and female alike, can have a fear of commitment in a relationship so that when the subject of moving in together or marriage comes up, one or the other may feel fear. The fear may be of losing their freedom or a fear of losing a person they have grown very attached to, or a fear of the change the commitment would bring.

If either one of this couple were to analyze the fear of commitment they would realize that they don't need to lose their freedom and they should not fear change because everything is always changing. Every second of every day we all are changing and moving forward.

If we are not moving forward we are moving backwards and we should be more afraid of moving backwards than forwards.

Fear can also be of moving out of your comfort zone into a new life or lifestyle. Take for example if you were to lose weight. That can be a huge fear as you are letting go of the person you have been for so long. You are afraid of moving out of your comfort zone, you have a real fear of losing the person you have created over the years and known maybe for your whole life. Once you realize you are afraid of letting go of the person you have been for so many years, that is half the battle won; you have taken back your power. Then you will need to take the time to grieve for the person you were.

During any transformation, be it in your body, mind or spirit, you need to take it one step at a time and to realize that you are going to hit the wall of fear several times during a transformation, because as you progress you are changing the person you know.

The person you once knew is getting further and further away and that can be scary.

You have to realize fear is just doing its job. If we did not have fear to move us forward step by step slowly, we would go rushing ahead without appropriate caution and most probably cause ourselves and others damage. Without fear, you would throw caution to the wind, but you might find you could really hurt yourself. So fear can be a very positive emotion, and a very good friend and guardian that takes care of you. But don't abuse the relationship you have with fear and use it as a cage; an excuse not to make a commitment or to change. There is a difference.

If you put out the energy that you use fear as a cage, you may put the energy out that you don't want to try, you just don't care, and you want to give up. Then you will begin to draw in like-minded people. The rut you were in will soon become much deeper and a lot harder to get out of.

Be aware of how you use fear on a daily basis and take back your power. Look for causes. Ask yourself what it is trying to teach you. Realize each emotion has a job and your emotions are there to help you.

Jealousy

Anger is cruel and destructive, but it is nothing compared to jealousy.

—The Good News Bible, Proverbs:

Chapter 27, Verse 4

As you change your life and things begin to improve you are going to find that this invokes some jealousy in others. Some people are very stuck in their belief systems; are not ready to change. Please be aware of this and the energy they will be putting out, that may infect you.

When we are jealous of another person we send them energy. We look at what they are doing and we want to be like them. When a person is jealous of another, they can actually see what they might be capable of obtaining themselves. This triggers an emotional response that offers an opportunity to clear a block; something from your past, perhaps even as far back as your childhood, that stops you progressing. Take for example if someone has ability and/or talent which you know that you could be capable of, but which, due to your beliefs, you have never developed. You wish that you could do what they do, and may, with that, feel jealousy, which is an emotional reaction to them. You may fear facing the truth about yourself as reflected in that person. On the other hand you start giving more energy to that person in the form of jealousy, because they are getting attention/energy as a result of their abilities or talents.

The more energy you feed your jealously the more energy goes to that person, and you may soon become irritated or frustrated to the point where you just blow up or boil over. You first find a change in their energy, the air about them has changed as they react to your energy. Then you may make comments to try to belittle them, or you may just start an argument with the person. These are intended to get your energy back.

In the worst cases of jealousy, energy can be restored by using excessive physical force. That is where jealousy can lead. Your energy drops further and further until you snap, at which point it becomes a matter of survival and you do everything and anything to get that energy back; create an argument – even lash out physically. This is not good!

The solution is simple. Realize you are experiencing feelings of jealousy. Be more aware of why you are acting jealously toward someone. Realize that the person who is the object of your jealously is just reflecting back to you who you really are inside. You may have hidden your true self away so well that you may even be in denial, but if you are jealous of someone that is your true self coming out and slapping you in the face and saying wake up.

For example, if you are jealous of someone's beauty it shows that you have beauty as well but for some reason you feel too vulnerable to be that beautiful person you truly are inside. You may associate beauty with drawing something bad in, so you don't want to face the fact that you are beautiful, and it is very easy to use jealousy to avoid dealing with the hurt and maybe even painful memories you associate with being beautiful. Everyone is beautiful in different ways but in this world today beauty is a very big emotional trigger and many people become very jealous over someone else's beauty.

Jealousy could also happen when you look to someone who has a great deal of money – who is financially secure – and think they are really lucky and you are just not that lucky. First you have sent out energy about money that is not altogether positive. The energy you just sent out about what you think about money or those who have it, has created your present reality. Then you may find you are jealous of people who have attained financial success. The thing is if you are jealous of that success, then you have inside of you the ability to attain the same or similar success in life. Jealousy toward a person you may see as successful is just a way of avoiding facing your own resistance toward change and to making a better life for yourself – in this case addressing how to attain financial success for yourself.

Your jealousy is an important signal to you. It is time to stop hiding the fact that you are afraid to become financially secure. Realize the reason you may be living your life this way is because of the energy you have put out, and the energy you put out is going to manifest. Anyone can achieve some form of success in their lives. There is nothing stopping them; just themselves and the energy they put out.

If you continue to be jealous of what others have, this is just the same message repeating itself over and over again. You are locked into the same life, same patterns, and no one can release you from these but you. It is all a matter of energy.

If you have feelings and/or emotions of jealousy toward a person, you are using the emotion in a way that does not benefit you, ~~to~~ and so you are resisting and blocking any change, so you can forever get to stay in a your comfort zone and what you may consider a safe place to be. Ongoing jealousy indicates that you are holding life at arm's length. Imagine holding your arms out in front of you right now, and that is what you do every time you feel jealousy, which is holding life at arm's length.

Now remember each emotion has a job to do and jealousy has one as well. When we bury a part of our true self inside us, jealousy will help bring it to the surface so that we can become our true self and bring to light the best we can be in this lifetime. Being your true self and being true to yourself is going to bring balance and calm into your life. Which creates a much happier and healthier you transforming your life for the better and so putting you in a healthier mindset to get the rewards you want and that may actually be waiting for you.

Patience

Patient persuasion can break down the strongest of resistance and can even convince rulers.

— The Good News Bible, Proverbs:

Chapter 25, Verse 15

Patience is the ability to wait. Impatience on the other hand, can be a self-sabotaging behaviour. So what happens when we can't wait, when we can't be patient? Why is it so important to be patient in life and what does it achieve? Let's look at what impatience achieves and you may understand why it is better to put out energy of patience instead of impatience.

Let's assume you have a goal or something you want. To get it you have to go through a process which requires some patience. You become impatient, for whatever reason and in so doing, create the energy of impatience. You are responsible for this feeling.

Impatience has a lot of emotion attached to it. When you have lots of unresolved emotions you tend to hold it in your body in the form of an energy block. With impatience, it is like that alarm clock is sounding all the time. Imagine the block you are creating. Hence, impatience is a self-sabotaging behaviour.

If you stand back and look you will realize that in being impatient, you are pushing away your goal. This suggests that on some level you feel you don't deserve what you wish to achieve; that which would bring you happiness.

For example, let's consider you want to find a soul mate. You would need to exercise a little patience to say the least. But people are not a patient lot at the best of times and today many people seem to want everything five minutes ago. When we decide we want something it must happen straight away at the very least.

What are you really saying when you want to meet your soul mate and it is not happening for you straight away? You create impatience with all the emotions attached to that, and an energy block which holds you back. Then you may start saying and doing things that are unappealing to others, that appear needy, or pushy, or dominating. These negatives then cloud over your many positive qualities, from the viewpoint of an external observer. Being impatient tends to drive someone or something away that you really want. In the case of wanting to meet your soul mate, being impatient is like chasing your soul mate away with a broomstick, and yelling as you go 'Don't you dare come anywhere near me!'.

People say 'I want to meet my soul mate, I really do!' and I am sure they truly believe that. But what they say on the one hand and do on the other are different. Being impatient, translates as 'Don't you dare bring my soul mate to my doorstep!'. You personally create impatience, so you are personally responsible for your present set of circumstances. You are responsible for meeting your soul mate or not meeting your soul mate; it is completely up to you.

When you are ready to change your energy toward meeting your soul mate, you will surely draw the right person to you at that right time in your life. I have seen people say they are patient about something but they are still putting out pretty scary energy. Remember, all the energy you put out toward meeting someone has to be something you also would be attracted to. Being patient is a very positive energy to put out.

So if you are impatient, how will you change? As the energy block of impatience grows and remains in the body, it may seem like it would be difficult to deal with after such a long time. I have good news; once you decide to clear this energy block, created by impatience, it can clear pretty quickly. The only thing that would stop you is a little thing called resistance. You can choose to resist or choose not to resist. If you are aware of being impatient and have this new understanding that impatience is resistance, you can then say to yourself you don't want this.

If you grasp this concept of patience, you will heal and move on very quickly. In time you will be able to clear other blocks, and it will be like hitting the ground running after that. Patience will become part of your everyday life and it won't be as trying as you may find it to start. You see what is really going on most excitingly: you are the master of your emotions and not a slave to them.

Another example where patience is a winner with regard to your personal transformation is for weight loss. Many people start exercise programmes and diet plans then say they don't work for them. Maybe in some cases they don't. But what I have found is that many people want results straight away – instant results. In truth, they need patience to achieve this.

To be impatient about any weight loss programme is to subtly say that you do not want weight loss. At the deeper level, you are resisting changing. When you lose weight, you change not only the outer you but the inner you and you need to exercise a little patience because you need time to adjust to the change. You are saying goodbye to an old friend you may have known for years – even a lifetime. You need time and patience to do this.

The job of patience is that it tells you what you want and what you really don't want. Patience tells you what you are ready to do right now. Impatience tells you that you may need a little more time to rethink those changes before you are ready for the change. Simple really; patience is very clear cut, telling you every day I really want this and I need a little more time to think about that. Understanding patience makes life very simple indeed.

Everything returns to what remains. Run after it, and you'll find it; sit patiently, and it will find you.

-Daniel Levin. The Zen Book

Boredom

In teaching, the greatest sin is to be boring.

—Chinese Proverb

Many of us are just so bored with life; you may hear others say *I'm so bored* or *I feel so bored and I don't know what to do*. Each emotion and feeling has a job to do and so does *boredom*.

When you feel bored, this is an emotional indicator to let you know it is time for a change, it is time to move out of your comfort zone again. This is the job of boredom, to let you know change is required.

Many get stuck in their boredom. What one actually does is they feed into the feeling of being bored. If you feed into any feeling or emotion you are choosing to not move forward but to stay where you are. Instead of feeding into boredom, look at your present situation, realize it is time for change and then move forward.

When someone is bored they may just sit at home in front of the television and do nothing. They may even say things like "I am too bored to go for a walk" and feed into the feeling of being bored. Then as a result they show no motivation to do anything, as they have just fed into the feeling of boredom. Some people can get bored with their exercise plan and it just becomes so routine and so boring. If you are bored with your exercise routine it is an indicator to change. It could be time to change your exercise routine and step it up to make it more fun or exciting or more challenging. Allow boredom to do its job and you may find that if you change your exercise plan you may not plateau but continue to lose weight and shape your new body the way you want it to and receive a very beneficial and rewarding outcome for yourself.

Another reason you could become bored with your exercise routine is because you need to change it so that you don't give up, or lose your motivation, or it could be that you just need to fool your body so your weight loss or improvements to your body form continues to progress instead of standing still. If you let boredom do its job you will find that you can maintain your motivation, your passion, your drive to push to achieve the body and form you have always desired. Next time you are bored, realize boredom has a job to do and let boredom do its job. Boredom means it is time for change, it is time to move out of your comfort zone. It is time to move forward. So next time you feel boredom coming on don't feed into this feeling of boredom, look around and see what your next step is and take it. Feed into your boredom and you won't know what your next step is on your life path.

Allow boredom to do its job and let it become an emotional indicator to tell you it is time to move out of your comfort zone even if in a small way. Let this emotional indicator of boredom keep pushing you forward so that you will be able to gain more opportunities to achieve your success in life.

Control

Control, or what I lovingly call being a 'control freak' is an interesting behaviour. It is one that is used to hide almost all of your emotions and feelings and anything that you do not want to deal with.

Being a control freak is also about hiding your true self from anyone else. If, however, you are not being your true self, then you can't be feeling very balanced. Keeping up such behaviour may cause a lot of discomfort in your life. The energy that goes into controlling all your emotions and feelings, hiding so much from everyone – including the people you care about – will drain your resources and your life force; your energy.

Control issues are generally trust and fear based. People with control issues do not trust others to do things, as they are downright scared that something will go wrong if they don't do it themselves. The fear is very real to them, so they really won't take the chance to trust another person, even with such an 'important task' as making a cup of coffee for them. People using control to suppress feelings and emotions usually first control everything in their personal lives, around the home, about themselves and then branch out to where they work. The need to control becomes like a substance abuse problem; they need to control more and more in and around their lives. Some may control their family, partners, children and even friends. They may even get very extreme and stop going anywhere or socializing in places they know they cannot control.

People with control issues tend not to want to stay away from home and they may buy more than one home so that they can go on holiday, as their need to control is very important to them. In the end, most, if not all people with control issues become reclusive because they need to control everything in and around them.

Do you know anyone like this? Or maybe you recognize yourself? Understand why a person needs to control. They are trying to minimize stimulation of their emotions and repressing those that do arise. Control is their way of coping with everyday life stresses. Being aware that one has a control issue is a start. Continuing to be aware is a major step on the pathway to try to heal the behaviour.

If you take control away from the life of someone who uses control to suppress their real self they will feel vulnerable and it will bring up many feelings and emotions. Often these will explode to the surface, though each person is different. In some experiences control is replaced by other problems; give up control and eat, or give up control but become a workaholic.

Simply being constantly aware of the need to control is how to clear it and it should clear very quickly. If it does not, there is still resistance in the form of a need to suppress or hide feelings and emotions and not deal with them.

I am sure you realize by now, that the energy you put out is the energy you get back. A control freak's energy levels will be right down from trying to keep it up. Imagine how much time and energy that needing to control is taking away from areas of your life like your partner, children, family and friends. Maybe you could give that time and energy to healing other areas of your life, achieving goals you could really benefit from. Wanting to control is a choice, needing to control is a choice, and being fully aware that you feel a strong need to control is also a choice. Being aware of your need to control is a very healing choice one that will bring you bliss and harmony.

Allow time to let go of your need to control as a lot of emotions and feelings will arise and getting in touch with your true self again can make you feel a little vulnerable. Give yourself time to grieve over the person you once were being the control freak, with any change you need to grieve. If you have been a controlling person then it is a behaviour that has been around for a long time and so you will need time to let the behaviour go, but also let the person you were go and embrace the new. Take some time and be a little gentle with yourself. In time you may find you won't need to control as much. At least you get to control this process and you can go as slow or as fast as you wish. Have a little faith, trust in yourself and stay aware. Being aware of your need to control and understanding this need is often all you need to overcome this behaviour.

If you are a control freak, *Who Stole My Energy?* is all about giving you back your control; not of others, but of yourself. Take what is in these pages and educate yourself in a new form of control, a healthier way to control; not using control to suppress feelings and emotions and anything else you don't want to deal with.

The less you suppress your emotions and feelings or anything you do not want to deal with, with your need to control, the more you will reap the rewards.

When you have no energy blocks from suppressing your emotions, with the use of control, your energy can flow as it naturally should. Rewarding you with more balance in your life as your body and energy flow starts to realign its self, and then filters out into all areas of your life.

Love

Over time, the word love has lost some of its power and its meaning. Many people may say things like 'I love the weather!', 'I love those shoes!', 'Love your car!', 'Love that outfit!' and so on. We use love so frivolously that its power has been diluted. When pushed into negative situations people start to say things such as, 'If you loved me you would do this!', or, 'How could you do that when you said you loved me?'

If many people stood around a giant white elephant and you ask them what it looked like they would each give you a different description depending on their viewpoint. Equally everyone has a different idea of what love is depending on their perception. Here is my white elephant, and I hope my understanding of love gives you another view. It may show you another way to get in touch with your true feelings of love.

When I personally feel love for someone it is a euphoric feeling that I feel inside. If you feel that euphoric feeling you will feel lighter and you will feel love; it is truly a beautiful emotion. I can feel this toward friends and family, even toward nature when I tune into the beauty of nature. I feel the lightness and the euphoric feeling and it lifts my spirit.

The euphoric feeling of love I feel toward another or to nature is also returned to me. It is not my intention to send this energy out to get something back. I just like the way it feels. I like what I see when I feel love.

When you are angry you know what that feels like; you probably recognize the signs straight away. You probably even know how to describe what it feels like to be afraid, happy, and sad but how many people truly and honestly know what it feels like to feel love – sent and received.

The job of love as an emotion is to bring the healing energy behind it. If you feel the euphoric feeling of love it will bring lightness to your very soul and a healing energy you may not be able to get any other way. Connecting to the feeling of love can calm you and a feeling of peace may come over you.

Connecting to this feeling of love – if you are really connected – the natural beauty around you every day will look brighter and more beautiful. I realize that it would take a lot of time and effort to stay connected like that every minute of every day, but when you do connect it is truly beautiful.

Love holds the hardest lessons of all because love unlocks all of life's mysteries.

— Renee Henderson

I wanted to share what I feel and see when I experience the euphoric feeling of love, because it is such a wonderful, beautiful and healing emotion. Of course there are people who mistake trust for love and patience for love though these are different again. I can understand this, because if you truly have felt love and that very light, euphoric feeling toward another person, then to give trust and respect and patience to the person you love should not be difficult at all.

I would like to take a moment to share something I wrote inspired by a friend I care for very much. I wrote this to a friend, with love ...

Hope is never enough to quench the thirst of a lonely heart. Fill the soul with love so no hope is ever required. Empty yourself of attachment, as it will only bring sorrow. Attachment is to go externally, giving your power away. Empower yourself, as one person can change so many. Be of this world and not a part of it.

Love is a breath of energy that should pass through you. It should not be caged or held, it is only to be felt. Love is what makes a sane man cry, for many try to capture this feeling of love. Allow the feeling of love to pass through you and so allow this feeling to heal a part of you.

Love holds a power all of its own, it can heal so much, make a heavy soul light. Love can hurt when one tries to hold it making the lightest of souls heavy. Love is a power we all know and to give and receive love is a gift. Love can heal if one will allow. Love has a gift wrapped up in an emotion, it will touch you, and the memory will linger, and this is your gift.

I was taught a long time ago if you are going to give a gift, give with your heart and never expect anything in return. If you give a gift of any kind and expect something in return this was a lie.

Love is a gift, if you decide to give the healing gift of love to someone then do not expect anything in return. If you do expect something in return then you never truly loved.

Hate

To hate another is to hate yourself.

We all live with the one Universal Mind.

What we think about another, we think about ourselves.

If you have an enemy, forgive him now.

Let all bitterness and resentment dissolve.

You owe your fellow man love;

show him love, not hate. Show charity and goodwill

toward others and it will return to enhance your

own life in many wonderful ways.

- Brian Adams. How to Succeed

To talk about *love* we have also to talk about *hate*, as there is a fine line that runs between these two emotions. I am sure you have heard of a *love/hate* relationship. *Love* and *hate* seem to run very close to one another.

Most of us look at hate as a very negative emotion. When you say 'I hate that!' or 'I hate that person!' we all recognize that such a statement is normally quite strong.

The surprising thing is, no one can seriously hate anything or another without first hating themselves; in some part, at least. The feeling and emotion of hate has a job to do. It is an opportunity to recognize that there is something that you hate about yourself and that you need to heal that part of yourself. Hate is a signpost in life to show you that you need healing. Using the word hate toward anything or anyone is an opportunity to heal. Take the sign and heal your own life.

Yes, hate can lead to some pretty nasty behaviour, but so can many other emotions if we do not set out to understand them and deal with them. If we don't express all our emotions and feelings including hate, and let them do their job then we will never have the opportunity to truly heal our emotions. What actually leads to the nasty behaviour related to hate, is the fact that you are feeding into the emotion instead of letting it do its job.

So many people give their power away to their emotions and they give away a lot of power to the emotion of hate. It is not a feeling that should be locked away. It is only locked away because many of us have associated so many negatives toward the feeling of hate. Understand hate instead. It is healthy to feel your emotions, all of them, but don't feed into them because then they become destructive.

Here is another thought about the emotion or feelings of hate that you have toward something or someone is that by hating you are creating an attachment to this object or person. Attachment to anything or anyone is not healthy.

Next time you use the word 'hate' realize you are attaching yourself to that object, person and memory. So next time this memory is triggered so is that attachment you created and you in turn will end up having overwhelming feelings of hate and even anger and you may wonder what sent you into this emotional tail spin.

Happiness/Good Humour

They say happiness is a state of mind, and what a great state of mind it is. Can you imagine the wonderful energy you put out with being happy? Good energy goes out so good energy comes back.

Happiness is also often associated with humor. But there is a light side and a dark side to humor. We can use humour in our everyday lives to lift our spirits, to make us and others feel good. But we can also use humor to hide behind; to play the class clown while hiding what we are truly feeling inside. The class clown entertains everyone yet often hides nervousness, shyness, feelings such as that they don't fit in, low self-esteem, poor ability and other such issues. They act up to gain acceptance.

They could actually be hiding personal pain and suffering. Just because they are children does not mean they don't suffer. Next time you see a child or an adult playing the class clown, don't dismiss them but be aware they are hiding behind their act.

Have you heard the term 'putting on a brave face'? Many do it and many use happiness to do it. They hide behind their smiles and what may seem like happiness but behind that humour may lie a lot of suppressed emotions and feelings going unsaid. It is a way of coping that some people use daily. They make jokes and are very entertaining but they are hiding what they are really feeling.

I have found that some people who hide behind their bravado or humour are very sensitive people, shy otherwise and very nice people. They are so sensitive that they create the class clown so that if people don't like that person, it doesn't matter as much because it is not really who they are. It is like; 'How can you hurt me when you don't even know me?' They do not feel safe to be themselves because of the hurt that may come as a result of them being their true self.

If someone hides their true selves behind humor or bravado they are just suppressing who they really are, to an extent at times that they may even lose touch with that person. They then lose touch with what they should really be doing with their lives. They may even lose sight of their life path and direction. They need to get back in touch with themselves so that they can live their true life and draw in a healthier energy.

The lighter side to humour and happiness is that when you are truly happy, it relaxes you. It takes away tension and it actually gives your body an opportunity to heal. Many people lead stressful lives and have all the stress related illnesses to go with it; tension in the shoulders that cause neck ache and headaches to ulcers and heart disease.

Happiness may not give you a complete cure for ulcers or serious health conditions but it is a wonderful addition to your healing process. As the saying goes; laughter is the best medicine and enjoying a good laugh is not only good for your health but it will relax you, which with most conditions where you suffer from pain, is known to help.

When we are truly enjoying humour, happiness and a good laugh think about the energy it is creating. How are you feeling? It is one of those times when you are putting out energy maybe without thinking about it, you are sending out happy energy and that is what will come back.

Each thought, feeling, emotion, word and action is energy, so imagine laughter and the feelings that go with it. That is what is coming back to you. Now that is a happy thought.

Happiness can set you free, it gives you a rest from all your worries and day-to-day stresses. For that moment when you are laughing and enjoying some form of happiness, the daily grind and stresses of the day melt away like magic. Humour can truly set you free and for that moment, life's burdens don't seem so heavy.

Humour, happiness and laughter have many jobs to do as you may have read. You can use humour to hide behind, use it as a form of healing, a form of relaxation or as a way to escape your life's burdens, even if only for a moment in time. Lastly, it is a way to draw in more positive and nurturing energy. The better the energy, the healthier you will be.

Abandonment

When you go through any personal transformation, you let go of part of you that you have known well. That, as we have said, can be tough. Abandonment is another emotion signalling to you that you have to do some 'work'; it also means that if you do work on it you are going to undergo some changes. When a person who you have known well for a long time leaves you for any reason, you may well feel vulnerable and abandoned on some level. Where you have lost someone you loved, who supported you, nurtured you and loved you in some way, it may feel like life has just ripped a rug from under you.

People who have once been abandoned often work hard to try to avoid experiencing that abandoned feeling again. They may try to make an unhealthy relationship work in the hopes of saving it, as losing it recreates those feelings of abandonment. Or they may go through life afraid of letting people get too close to them, because if they get too close and then leave it kills them a little more inside. If you already suffer from a fear of abandonment due to someone you cared about leaving you, then you need to understand such feelings so they can lose their hold on you.

Another sign of abandonment is always leaving someone before they can leave you. Leaving jobs before you outstay your welcome or become too attached are also examples. You may say your work is not challenging, or that it is boring, as you need an excuse to leave your work before you become too attached to it with consequent feelings of vulnerability and possible abandonment.

The sign of abandonment you may recognize most easily, is that you may enter then leave relationships 'before it is too late'. The relationship could be going just fine and then the self-sabotaging begins. In the relationship you start to pick at every little thing, having arguments over nothing. When you have little arguments over nothing, more times than most it is masking a bigger problem. In the case of a fear of abandonment you create these little arguments so you have a way out of the relationship. You need an out because the person is getting too close and the closer they get the more fearful you get of being abandoned.

To get the sense of freedom back and to feel strong again you need to understand these feelings and why you do these things and heal your abandonment fears in order to be able to have a happy and secure relationship. This applies to all relationships, marriages and friendships. People with abandonment fears won't get too close to friends, as letting someone in makes them feel vulnerable. To feel powerful again, and to retain control of their lives they tend to find little things to pick at to drive their friends away. Once the friends are gone they feel stronger again. The friends don't realize that they were driven away because of fear that they would get too close and then abandon them. To a sufferer of abandonment issues, the pain seems far worse to be abandoned than to drive a friend away. The upside to this fear is that most people who suffer from fear of abandonment can hit the ground running when it comes time to heal. They are so used to leaving to avoid getting hurt, that changing is as natural as any other habit in their lives. Yes, it may hurt a little but someone with abandonment issues can turn it around very quickly and seem to bounce back very smartly. It does not mean they are heartless, they bounce back so fast because if they don't that means they will have to face their fears. And no one actually likes feeling vulnerable.

People with abandonment issues have a fear of commitment so it is very difficult to get any kind of commitment out of them. I would say more times than most they don't marry until they are much older by which time they feel calmer and more at peace with themselves; able to trust themselves enough to take this step. That or they feel they have healed enough and are strong enough to risk abandonment again.

Many people with abandonment issues may fear commitment not so much because of the commitment itself but because of the fact that they know that they will indeed get very close to someone and then due to their expectations they may be abandoned.

I say 'due to their expectations', because being abandoned is something they expect will happen, in which case they draw it in more times than most. Then their worst fears are realized and vulnerable feelings return, possibly putting them off relationships for life.

The mind is incredibly powerful. Expectations of any kind are equally powerful. What you expect in life you get; it is as simple as that. If you expect a bad outcome you tend to draw that into your life. If there is another person involved and you expect a bad outcome, you greatly affect that person in a negative way. As expectations of abandonment draw it to you more times than most, be totally aware of what your expectations in life really are.

Feeding into your Emotions

It is far better for you to control your attitudes and feelings than to have them control you.

-David Baird. A Thousand Paths to tranquillity

Each emotion has a job to do such as the feeling of anger is fear based, meaning when you become angry a feeling of fear or feeling vulnerable has triggered this emotion of anger. Boredom is another emotion that has a job and that is to indicate it is time to make a change or move out of your comfort zone.

Be aware of feeding into an emotion: imagine someone becomes angry and instead of asking themselves what has made me feel vulnerable, and allowing the emotion of anger to do its job, they feed into it the emotion of anger. When someone feeds into anger it can result in the anger escalating and maybe causing harm to one's self or another person.

This is what feeding into an emotion can do. All emotions are healthy, feeding into an emotion is not healthy.

When you feed into any emotion or feeling you are blocking your progress, you are avoiding something, resisting moving forward.

Feeding into your emotions is going to create a lot of confusion, and once you have lost clarity you have lost your clear view of your life path. If you have no view of your path, you have no direction and you will find yourself in the dark with what seems like no way out and no end to the obstacles that will seem to roll into your life.

What is so wrong with feeding into your emotion? You could be saying I have done that for years. But if you want to get what you have always got, then continue to feed into your emotions and block yourself achieving your goals, avoid and resist any changes. But if you want to have more in your life – be it change, success, improved health and well-being, then stop feeding into your emotions and feelings.

Then next stop feeding into experiences, life situations that come up that seem difficult. Maybe you are in a relationship that isn't working and you make excuses, and see the relationship through rose-tinted glasses. Someone has the strength and courage to tell you the truth and you create a drama to feed into it. You make a mountain out of a mole hill and blow everything out of proportion and you have created something that you can now feed into so you don't have to face the truth about your relationship, or about anything you don't want to deal with or look at.

There are some people who are quite ill and maybe in pain and they feed into the illness and pain and all the emotions attached. Using the illness, pain and emotions as a way to avoid change, success and moving forward or even achieving the goals they say they want to achieve. The illness and pain is fed into and becomes a crutch and an excuse not to be involved in anything and everything. Feeding into an illness is a great way to hide away from others and the world so you don't have to get on with your life.

The more someone feeds into their pain and illness the worse it can make it, and making it all very hard to manage one's pain levels or the conditions of their illness. I realize there are people out there who have real pain and real illness that are painful and at times frustrating. Then you have people who have illnesses that other people can't even see, and don't get understood. Many people in this lifetime are given crosses to bear and it is up to them if they want to feed into the pain and frustration and all the feelings and emotions connected to this; it is their choice to avoid growth, and successful change. If they do not feed into the emotion or illness and/or pain and step back and take the time to understand why this is happening and understanding this was given to them for a reason, they will realize they have been given an amazing opportunity to learn and gain knowledge and wisdom others may never have an opportunity to obtain.

If this triggers you or you have some emotional response, then there is something that needs to be seen and learnt. Then understand I would never talk about such a subject unless I had helped others who were in pain or live with some form of ill health. Then take it one more step further in understanding, and know every day I live in physical pain; it may not be visible to others but I live with pain every day. My ill health and pain was once the heaviest of all my burdens and now it is my greatest Teacher and Healer.

A wise friend once told me that not all illnesses are meant to be healed or taken away from a person, as so much learning, knowledge and wisdom can be gained from such a Teacher as illness.

Our journey through life may not always seem perfect, and the road may not always be straight but with some understanding and compassion not only for others but for yourself, your burdens can be made lighter. With the lightening of your burdens success will soon come into view and soon within your grasp.

At times people feed into their emotions and the dramas of life. I have seen many people do this a few times and one I have found is very popular is when someone wants to lose weight.

They say they want to lose weight but they create emotions like impatience and feed into it. They may constantly say *they are huge or fat, or overweight, and they can't do it as it is just too hard,* and they are physically upset when they express themselves, feeding into the emotions. Remember feeding into your emotions is resistance, avoidance to change. When a person feeds into their emotions over wanting to lose weight they set themselves up to overeat, binge, or what is best known as emotional eating.

Emotional eating is suppressing your feelings and of course your emotions; also you suppress anything you do not want to deal with. Allowing your emotions to do their job in the first place may allow you to stop feeding into the emotions and then you would not feel the need to suppress.

When you feed into an emotion you are actually avoiding change and success. If you are constantly feeding into your emotions and not allowing your emotions to do their job, you are holding up your own success. Realizing you are feeding into your emotions will get you one step closer to achieving success and your personal or professional goals in your life.

Awareness is important, as being aware of when you are feeding into an emotion, illness, pain, life experience, weight loss, lifestyle change, is going to mean that you can see what you are trying to avoid and you can get yourself back on path. When you can see what you are avoiding, you can understand more of why you are doing this and as a result of this understanding you regain your clarity.

Then you may find life was not as hard as you once thought as feeding into your emotions is creating speed-bumps, pot-holes, ruts to slow you down. It is your choice how fast or slow you want to move along your life path. So it is also your choice how fast or slow you want to achieve success in your life.

Think of all the time you would save not feeding into your emotions, it is about working smarter not harder. If you are working smarter, success may find its way to you a lot sooner.

Emotional Triggers

Believe nothing, no matter where you read it or who has said it, not even if I have said it unless it agrees with our own reason and your own commonsense

—BUDDHA

I wondered how some emotions seem to runaway with us and at the end of the emotional outburst or reaction we are left wondering what just happen. Then you may beat up on yourself, be hard on yourself about how you reacted to something that seemed so simple once your mind cleared. This is when I began to learn about emotional triggers.

An emotional trigger is for a quick example, you hear a song on the radio and you bypass thought and burst into tears and become very emotional. Then if you are aware you will realize that it was a song that you listened to on the last holiday you spent with a loved one just before they passed, or it could be from another memory that hurts just as deep or maybe it was a happy memory.

When something happens to us that created a strong emotion this creates an emotional trigger, so when you hear a word, come across a similar situation that is familiar to you this releases an emotional trigger. The bigger the outburst the more painful the past event may have been for you, or it could be that it took so long for you to recover from this past situation, whatever the painful situation was and then the time to recover or rather suppress is a pressure cooker turned up on high and always dangerously close to exploding and sometimes not in the healthiest of ways.

For some people that have been abused in their childhood or sometime in their lives maybe for many years and then there is the years of so called recovery which is really suppressing the pain as the pain of abuse never goes away. So when they come across a person that abuses their position of power in the workplace over you, or you come across abuse in a friendship or relationship, up comes the emotional trigger and you may even go right back to that age of when you experienced the painful event that took place and your guard goes up, or you shut down, or there is a huge emotional outburst. Sometimes there is too much to wade through that this particular emotional trigger causes you to maybe even mentally breakdown, 'enter Depression', I am not diagnosing here I am just pointing out a pattern I have seen and even experienced firsthand.

For some abuse at anytime of your life is a very deeply ingrained emotional trigger because the abuse happen over many years and or it took many years of suffering to get something that resembles some kind of life of sorts.

I believe when someone is seriously abused that the abuser has robbed that person of a chance of a life, of happiness and a sense of feeling whole. People rape other people as it is the closest they can come to killing a person and I have heard someone admit to such a thing. People who abuse take away a life they kill a person's soul and create emotional triggers that can make life more difficult for the people who have been abused. But now they are aware of emotional triggers the people who have been abused or raped or worse have a way of dealing with a painful pass, it is just about being aware and being gentle with yourself and realize it may have taken years of your life, so give it time for you to be more aware of these emotional triggers and you may be able to take back more of your life.

Yes, I am passionate about helping people who have been through painful experiences or abuse of any kind I believe it is incredibly wrong.

Another emotional trigger I thought of is I cannot stand it when someone calls another person 'fat'. It is like calling a gay man a fagot which in my eyes is incredibly rude and abusive to gay men. I grew up with a younger brother that picked on two of my four sisters and he called them fat all the time and torturing them to the point of tears. When he grew up in years to what we call adulthood he told me he thought he was helping them. This I find very hard to believe as I remembered his tone and delight in making them cry when he called them fat.

So I have an emotional trigger when it comes to hearing the word 'fat' when describing a person and thanks to Auckland Hospital saying 'she/he is large' is another trigger. If someone is overweight, be compassionate and not torture them. I have heard in Hospitals medical professionals using these words and they are causing more harm than good. Remember, first do no harm.

One thing I have learnt is if I am personally overweight I am left alone by most men and I get on well with my female friends and females in general and I am taken seriously. Then when I am just at what I consider a lighter weight some men throw themselves at me in such rude and horrible ways, grab at personal parts of my body and I am talking about walking down the main street in the CBD. I get abused walking pass working sites where there are men. I have men asking me to dance when I go out with friends and if when I say no thank you, they get angry and upset, I remember one man yelled at me 'I don't want to have sex with you! I just want to dance with you!' What an ego, what he did not care to wonder a guess or to try and understand was the fact I suffer from a very painful health condition called Fibromyalgia and as much as I love to dance I can't enjoy this as much or not at all and yet if I was what they call overweight I would not have any of these problems. Other problems that come from being at a lighter weight is my female friends & other females become insecure and jealous of me and even attack me. I also get thrown dirty looks for being a lighter weight. And of course because I am a lighter weight I have no brain, not stereotype, fact. I have observed this in other people and from my own personal experiences.

Can you see all the emotional triggers on both sides of the fence? Be you overweight or a lighter weight you can't win, people have too many hang ups and emotional triggers. Whatever weight you choose to be, then be happy with it and accept yourself completely and do not use hurtful and insensitive remarks when you judge another person, it could come back to bite you when you least expect it and from someone you least expect. Think of this, the person you hurt today maybe the person that will be able to help you or a loved one later, your actions today matter and can create emotional triggers for you.

Say for some reason you get very sick or hurt and you cannot exercise, gain weight and or you become depressed or worse than one of your emotional triggers will become being called 'fat' and all those insensitive remarks will come back to haunt you as emotional triggers. It is something to consider and I believe that many who abuse people for being overweight fear this will happen to them. I was told by a lovely Nurse in Auckland Hospital that no one can avoid getting sick, everyone gets sick.

When you begin to be more aware and keep a map of your emotional triggers and you are aware of where they came from you know you have put yourself on the road to recovery, and a journey to healing.

Healing emotional triggers is about the journey and realizing it is a major healing. If you were to go into Hospital for major surgery would you expect to get up a few days later bouncing around feeling better, more like months before you could bounce on a trampoline or the like. So the message here is to be gentle with yourself as you become aware of your emotional triggers.

Also remember to be gentle with friends, family or a partner as they may not be aware of emotional triggers, something you could share with them once they have calmed down. And always ask can I share an insight I read about called emotional triggers and see where you go from there.

There was another emotional trigger I wanted to share it happen to a young boy who is now an adult. He was an altar boy for a Catholic Church and the Priest came to see him to give him envelopes and told this young boy to give them out. The young boy explained I cannot do this as my parents are taking us all away on holiday. The Catholic Priest didn't listen and told him to go around to all the houses and give the envelopes out. The money that would be donated in these envelopes would go to the Priest so it was important to the Priest. The young boy went straight home after school as directed by his parents and they went away for the weekend. When they got back the young boy went out tired and tried to post as many envelopes as he could. Now you have to realize this young altar boy was no older than 10 years old or younger. When the young boy went to school at the beginning of the week the Priest came into the young boys classroom and asked him to come up to the front of the classroom in front of children of all ages and the Catholic Priest beat the boy so badly that the male School Teacher / Principal of the School fainted. It left this young boy with an emotional trigger that followed him into his adulthood and so when confronted with you said you were going to do this that or the other, the now male adult lies and begins to twist the truth as that is his emotional trigger coming up. The now male adult emotional trigger makes him feel he is in the same situation again when he was the young altar boy and he told the truth then and that got him a beating, that no one helped him deal with then, so now when triggered he lies so nothing seriously bad will happen. When this male adult had this breakthrough with me he became emotional and his chest began to hurt, a reaction to the beginning of a healing that was well overdue.

So as you can see being aware of emotional triggers can be incredibly healing and helpful. Being aware when an emotional trigger comes up can mean taking back your life and living it the way you wish without fear of being beaten, abused or punished or worse. Remaining aware of emotional triggers will mean in time that your emotions may not just runaway with you.

Chapter 3   Self Talk

Be careful what you say and protect your life.

A careless talker destroys himself.

—The Good News Bible, Proverbs:

Chapter 13, Verse 3

What you say, has so much power. What you say manifests into your reality. The word is far more powerful then people realize. The energy of a word is so powerful, there is so much history behind each word and so it is not just your energy behind each word but energy from many years and even centuries. So a word carries so much power and punch, and so imagine the energy that comes with each word and this is the energy you put out and as a result draw back into your life. In this chapter you will understand what I mean by self talk, gain knowledge of its constructive and destructive power, and understand how damaging or helpful it can be to your energy and see how to turn your self talk into another powerful tool to regain your energy.

Much of what we say every-day actually goes unseen. Our everyday gossip and idle conversation often goes unseen. But it is the unseen language of self – and your inner talking to yourself – that draws so much into our lives yet we don't even recognize it. I call this unseen language the language of self talk.

We may wonder why we are not getting what we want, or why we are not moving in the right direction or even why we cannot find a direction. What invisible force is stopping us? One of these invisible forces may be the unseen language we speak every day; a language we don't even notice anymore. If we can't see it or even know about it, then how can we remedy it? To be better equipped to help ourselves, we have to be much more aware of this unseen language.

So what unseen language do we speak every day? Consider someone who goes around telling people 'I am confident' or 'I am beautiful, stunning, gorgeous'. People who need to say 'I am confident' are usually trying to convince themselves that they are confident. If you truly are a confident person then you won't have to say it; you will naturally give off the air and energy of someone who is confident.

If you are truly feeling beautiful, stunning and gorgeous, you shouldn't feel a need to tell people. If you feel that need, you might want to look a little deeper and you will find there lies within a very insecure person who really doesn't think they are as beautiful as they say they are. Beauty comes not only from appearance but from the inner beauty of the soul, and if you feel you do not have this beauty you may find a need to tell everyone you are beautiful just to convince yourself. When you hear yourself giving yourself praise then be aware why you are doing it. We are our greatest teachers and students, and so much knowledge waits within us all.

I have heard people who are spiritual say 'I am not in the ego'. I ask myself why do they feel a need to say this all the time. If they are truly without ego they won't need to advertise it. You won't need to make such statements unless you truly do not believe it yourself, or you need convincing to keep yourself on the right track. However you can be aware of your own self talk and the different ways you do use it and could use it.

Next time you hear yourself or another person say a bold statement about themselves, then remember that you need to look a little deeper. Take the opportunity to learn. Everything is a lesson. Everything is an opportunity to elevate.

Affirmations and Unseen Affirmations

The tongue is the cause of prosperity or poverty.

The tongue, again, is responsible for promoting friendship and kinship, for attachment and bondage, and for death and liberation.

—Sri Sathya Sai Baba

Many people may be familiar with affirmations and may have used them in their lives or are presently using them. An affirmation is basically a set of words or declaration you say to yourself often enough so that you gradually convince yourself that they are true and draw them to you.

I personally believe affirmations can work for people. Words are energy and everything you say and think becomes your world, your life and your reality.

Some people who have tried using such affirmations to better themselves, though, have found they haven't worked. So why does this happen?

If you want to use affirmations to draw healing, love, money, relationships and success into your life – just to name a few – you need to be fully aware all of the time. You need to stay completely aware of all your thoughts, words and actions for an affirmation to work.

You may, for example, put an affirmation out to say, speed up your metabolism so you can lose weight. But if you do not stay aware of it during the day, then by mid-morning, or by the time lunch comes around, you may have said, thought or done something to cancel out that affirmation.

For an affirmation like speeding your metabolism up, you might say it before bed and first thing in the morning. If you then go and pass a mirror or a reflection of yourself later during the day and judge yourself in a negative way this will cancel out your affirmation. With just a negative look or thought or word you have changed the energy of the affirmation.

I have said that you can't cancel out any energy you send out and that is true. If you send out a positive affirmation/energy you will get it back. But if you send out a negative one straight after it, you will also get that returned to you. So what you get is one step forward, one step back. All energy has to come back.

It may seem like a simple solution – say an affirmation and just be aware of your thoughts, words and actions. But it is not that easy; people have so many thoughts running through their heads daily. This starts as soon as you wake up in the morning, and right through to the evening. Many people also take several of their thoughts to bed with them at night. That must be crowded. No wonder people who think too much before bed don't get a good night's sleep or wake feeling un-rested.

Your mind never stops. If you actually relax your mind by emptying it out completely before bed you may find you sleep a lot better. But it is a near impossible task for many, so don't expect to get it straight away. Try to do this, however, because it will help the staying power of the affirmation.

"Then there is silence of the mind. The mind is a bundle of thoughts and fancies. These thoughts have to be reduced gradually. When thoughts are reduced, the mind naturally comes under control, like a clock that is unwound. When the activity of the mind is reduced, the power of the Atma (Self) manifests itself.

As a consequence, the intellect becomes more active than the senses."

—Sri Sathya Sai Baba

It doesn't have to be before bedtime that you make an affirmation; it can be at any time you choose. However if you want to draw into your life what you want then you might want to take the time first to clear your mind.

Why is clearing your mind so important? Imagine a pool of water. You drop a stone into the pool of water and it creates ripples. The ripples move out to the side of the pool and come back, just like energy does. Now imagine dropping hundreds of stones into the water and imagine the effect on the water's surface. Now imagine the energy that is coming back to you in a similar situation. You can't keep track of that, you don't know what is coming or going in your life and you may become overwhelmed, which leads to an imbalance in you and your life. There may be no calm in your life due to so many stones being dropped into the pool of water every day. Think of your age in days. How many stones have you dropped into the pool of water over those days? How many of those ripples have come back to you and are still returning to you? You are responsible for those stones. You are responsible for those ripples of energy coming back to you.

Once you have the awareness of your thoughts, words and actions, you will be able to have a little more control over what comes into your life and what you can draw in with affirmations and what you say daily. Please remember all this is not going to happen over night; you have several years of programming to undo. But if you are being fully aware of your thoughts, words, actions and even facial expressions then you should notice a difference, even if just in a small way. But you will notice the change start happening straight away.

Know that your unseen affirmations you speak every day – even with a friend over lunch – are still you dropping a stone in a pool of water. The ripples will return to you. Be aware so that you can stop and think; 'Should I really think that or say that? Do I really want that ripple returning back to me?'

Affirmations work, so make them work for you. You have been a slave to your own unseen affirmation, your unseen language you speak every day. Become completely aware and you will become a master.

I'm Only Joking

A man who misleads someone and then claims that he was only joking is like a madman playing with a deadly weapon.
—The Good News Bible, Proverbs: Chapter 26, Verses 18-19

Talk can be constructive or soul destroying for everyone involved. Many people can say something hurtful at times then make light of it, suggesting that because they made a joke of it, the bad behavior is okay and no harm is done.

How many people do you know say something and then say; 'But, I was only joking!' or who smile and otherwise indicate that they were joking? For example, I have seen such banter feature between couples at dinner parties, their strong criticisms often masquerading as light-hearted teasing.

It doesn't matter what is said: you really can't take it back. The hurt inflicted has hit its mark and the damage has been done. But they didn't really mean to insult you, or put you down because they were actually just joking, right? Wrong! This could not be further from the truth.

Everything that you say to another is meant for that person, be it suppressed feelings of anger toward that person, jealous feelings toward that person or whatever other feelings that have been suppressed. Once it is let out of the bag, so to speak, it needs to be cleared. Once an insult or a negative or destructive remark is out, there is no taking it back. But, with the comment out, this is an opportunity to clear a block that may be stopping your friendship or relationship from taking a step forward. We are here to learn and to elevate together. If we are not doing that, then we are not moving forward and so we end up holding one another back; sometimes one more than the other.

People who say; 'But I was only joking,' are 'chickening out' of taking responsibility for how they truly feel about that person or situation. It is time to face the truth and reality in its raw state.

First, be aware that many people who say hurtful things under the guise of a joke, are suppressing a lot of their own emotions and feelings – a lot of everything really. Over time, the weight of suppressing so much is like having the pressure of a freight train moving at full speed pressing against them. They try to hold it back but something has to give and in the end it always does, one way or another. The comment is made, but then quickly disguised as a joke, to minimize offence.

Once a remark is made, you might ask that person if they are willing to look at where that remark has truly come from. It will lighten their load and you may learn a lot from the situation; maybe even gain an opportunity to elevate, which is always a plus.

If you are the person who insults and then says 'I am only joking', start being more aware of the times you do it and then pull yourself up right there on the spot. Once an insult is out, so is the energy. You can't take energy back with an, 'I'm just joking'. It doesn't work that way; you can't cancel energy out. When you insult another or put someone down, you have sent out a negative energy.

The next step in pulling yourself up is being aware that you cannot insult another person and not realize that this is actually how you feel about yourself. Remember, when you judge another, be it in a good way or in a negative way, that is how you really feel about yourself. The insult more times than most is more directed at yourself than at another person. Either way you are going to have the energy returned to you.

You see there are no accidents in life. If you are meant to say something, you were meant to say it. There is no 'Oops I didn't mean it!' or 'Hey I was only joking!' But they are all opportunities.

Life is full of butterflies and blessings. How you see them is up to you. You can see things as obstacles or opportunities. Many of us see them as obstacles. It is easier to believe in the negative. That is why negative energy is so easy to put out and get back, because many do it so often and have done it for so long. Any habit can be hard to break so why expect breaking this habit to be easy? Persevere and in time, maybe, you will find your life is always filled with butterflies.

Everything in life is part of the plan; there is a blueprint to understanding life. We may all interpret this blueprint in our own way and manoeuvre through life differently, but whatever way we get through life, one thing will always remain the same – there are no accidents in this life.

Something I have shared with many is this, when you say something and then say 'I was just joking' I tell them remember there is 80% truth to what you just said. It is amazing how that particular statement sticks with people. To realize what they said and have tried to take back holds truth to it on some level for them.

The 'self talk' of saying 'I was only joking' – whether you are saying it or receiving it – is an opportunity to grow. Take the time to grow from it. Create another energy that you will actually look forward to receiving.

Chatterbox

A chatterbox is someone who loves to talk about themselves. One may think they are just full of themselves, or stuck in the ego. If you think this, you might be surprised to find that you are well off the mark.

There are many people who will talk your ear off. Some may actually be lonely, but in many cases the reason is this; the more they talk about themselves, the further they push you away. In fact you probably often tune out chatterboxes without even thinking about it.

When someone talks about themselves so much, you are not about to ask them any more questions. That would only make them talk about themselves even more. You may just want them to be quiet for a moment. So the more they talk, the less you are going to ask them about themselves, and they achieve what they need to – you not asking any questions.

Chatterboxes may talk a lot but consciously or subconsciously they are very secretive people. They tell you what they want you to know and that is it. It is actually a controlling behaviour that works rather well, especially because so many people are not aware of what some chatterboxes are doing. It is a wonderful way of keeping people out of your private life and at arm's length.

Chatterboxes talk about themselves, yet hidden behind this chatter is a person you really don't know. They may even be hiding something they really don't want you or anyone else to know about.

If you are a chatterbox do be aware that you are giving away too much precious energy. Because you are focusing on the person you are talking to, your energy is going to that person and draining you.

Once you feel the energy is starting to drain from you during one of your marathon conversations you may find you will become irritated, frustrated, impatient and even angry with the person you have been chatting to.

Being a constant chatterbox will drain you and you will feel vulnerable. You may resort to taking on a more powerful energy (eg irritation, anger, frustration) to get your energy back. Just remove yourself from the situation or the person whom you have been talking to and take some quiet time until your energy levels come back up, you may need to eat and/or sleep as you will feel exhausted and tired.

Every day conversations aren't the only thing that constitutes being a chatterbox. It is also the conversations about work and business that you use to hide yourself behind, keeping that vulnerable feeling at bay. That is not being a chatterbox surely? It is.

I am sure business talk is very important, but when is enough, enough? People on the receiving end of these business conversations may think you are dedicated and so very helpful. But the truth of the matter may be for you that this is just another way for you to avoid dealing with any kind of personal conversation and maybe even avoid going home and dealing with your own problems and personal life.

You may even find during or as a result of these business chats, that you feel stronger and you most probably do. If you are the one actually being the centre of attention you will be receiving energy from anyone who is giving you their focus. You may feel you are getting high on life and the thing is you really are. But what happens to the energy of the people sitting across from you? They become drained, grumpy, tired and all the emotions they will feel as they instinctively try to preserve their own energy levels.

The sad side to being a chatterbox is no one actually gets to know the real you. You may be waiting for someone to get to know the real you and you may even be annoyed by the fact that no one 'gets' you or understands you.

If you belong to the elite group of chatterboxes then realize you have a choice. Be aware of when you are chattering away and see if you can work out why you do it, especially if it is only in certain situations. Let other people get to know the real you or continue to remain in your comfort zone but do realize if you remain in your comfort zone you will always get what you have always got. If you are not a chatterbox then I hope this has enlightened you a little about people you know who love to talk all the time. It is their way of coping with life. Everyone has a way of coping and suppressing anything they don't want to deal with and this is just another one. Next time you talk to a chatterbox, talk to them about themselves and ask some questions. If they are safe questions they will answer. If you find the ones they are trying to hide they will change the subject quick smart and may even get very sharp with you, so realize that this is a possibility. You may not think it, but some chatterboxes really are very sensitive people you will find, so tread carefully. However you may find that your efforts to get to know this other person culminate in some wonderful surprises about them.

Lies

You have to hate someone to want to

hurt him with lies.

Insincere talk brings nothing but ruin.

—The Good News Bible, Proverbs:

Chapter 26, Verse 28

The lies we tell ourselves are so many that we may not even be able to recognize the truth any more. Through the lies we tell ourselves we may even have lost sight of who we really are. When you look in the mirror can you actually say with absolute honesty that the person staring back is your true self, not the image or product of many lies twisted and turned, so you could fit into the world and into what you see as how society wants you to look and act?

With the lies we tell ourselves we may even convince ourselves that we are living a life that we love and enjoy; that everything is okay, when deep down we feel a void and know something is missing inside of us. That void, that if filled would bring more calm and balance into your life, comes from who you really are; the intuition. Those inner feelings tug away at you sometimes, keeping you in check. By listening to them we can stop ourselves from going over the edge.

Lying to yourself is actually destructive. 'Who is it hurting?' you may ask. 'Just me, and no one else!' You might actually have convinced yourself that the lies you tell yourself are okay and that there is nothing wrong.

Lying to yourself is an energy you put out, and that energy permeates every part of you. If you lie to yourself you may not be able to reach those goals you want so much. If you lie to yourself how can you expect to find people who are going to be honest with you? People will react to the energy you are putting out and lie in return. How can you expect your partner or close friends to be honest with you? Put lying energy out there and it comes back from everyone and anyone, including your friends, family and loved ones; even from a stranger in a shop up the road. Wouldn't you rather people be honest with you, than dishonest? It is always your choice.

Remember energy that goes out comes back but it may not be packaged the way you like when the energy returns. You might have the lying energy returned to you as others feeling that they can't trust you so you miss out on opportunities that mean you don't get to fulfill certain goals you set yourself. You may get the energy back as people being negative toward you, because lies are really not that positive.

People say 'Everyone lies' and, 'White lies are okay because they save face, and save people's feelings.' There is no gray area here. Lies are lies and each is destructive. Whether you speak outright lies or white lies or you lie to yourself, a lie is a lie; period.

Why do so many people think white lies are okay? A friend expects that you are being honest with them. You may tell a white lie to protect their feelings or to delay their feelings being hurt, but this does not make it okay. If people are honest with one another we could all move forward a lot faster in life.

White lies are just wasting a lot of time and energy that could be invested another way. Okay, being honest with someone does not give license to be harsh and blunt with people. Being honest with someone is an opportunity to help, so be gentle and deliver the message they need to hear to help them.

If you go out shopping and a friend tries on an outfit you think does not suit them, realize that yours is just one person's opinion. A third person may actually like what they have tried on. When your friend asks whether the outfit looks nice on them you tell them the truth as you see it, explaining that yours is just one person's opinion and suggesting a second opinion is sought. You might also say that it is really up to them; they are going to wear the outfit so if they feel comfortable and confident in it, let them trust their own heart and intuition. These are ways of being honest without being plain blunt and harsh. But if they insist on hearing your opinion, then by all means tell them the truth, but again say this is just one person's opinion. If you are gentle with your friend you have created a gentle energy to come back to you, and there is your reward.

Now let's look at exaggerations these are also lies. At one time or another we have probably all exaggerated the facts to make ourselves sound good. Exaggerating makes us look good and the better we look, the more focus we get and hence the more energy.

Maybe you don't even realize you are doing it anymore because we all exaggerate so often who really notices or cares? But everything is energy and it will come back. Energy takes everything as fact so when you exaggerate, the energy just takes it as another negative energy or self-destructive energy and sends it right back. You are in charge of the energy. You have absolute control of that energy. Do you really want another serving of negative energy in return?

Think about another completely different energy like stress. You stress over something and the energy doesn't know any better; it just does as it is told and it gives you back exactly what you asked for – more stress. It is the truth. If you stress about money issues then the energy is going to give you more money problems to stress about. Very black and white but that is the world of energy; this is actually the world we live in. Maybe you will think twice about stressing over something now, as you come to understand that stress is not that healthy on the body or mind. Remember every little bit of knowledge helps and heals.

Now back to the exaggerating. By exaggerating you make yourself seem better than how you believe others see you, so you become a predator for energy. People who become envious, maybe even jealous, focus on you and you begin to receive energy as a result; not the healthiest way to receive, but it works. Actually telling any lie is making you a predator in one way or another, but you are the one who gets hurt in the end. Now that you are aware you may decide you don't want to punish yourself or self-sabotage your own life path which would bring that little more balance back into your life and life will start looking a lot clearer.

Exaggerating and telling any kind of lie is really very exhausting. You end up with so many balls to juggle in the air; it can't be easy. It must be very exhausting indeed. Juggling so many lies in your life, you might find you are tired all the time; one of many side effects of being drained of energy. Because you are so tired, other goals have to wait a little bit longer.

The solution to this is start being honest; not blunt, not harsh, but gradually start gently telling the truth and it will grow on you. Be sincere. Be sincere to yourself and to others. You will find your energy levels start to improve and you may find you are not so exhausted any more.

I hope you are starting to realize just how much control you have over your own life and start taking back your power and control. Remember that life was never meant to be hard. Our lack of knowledge and of insights about life have made it that way. There are so many paths home in this lifetime and we get to choose which one. As always it is your choice.

Confidence

Confidence is a language in itself. When someone is confident, they become a magnet for everyone though they may either be liked or disliked, depending on whether other people have triggers or blocks to do with confidence. People who are confident are noticed straight away. Confidence seems like an unseen force, or language. A confident person walks in and people cannot miss them; they seem to have a presence – an air – about them.

If you are not confident, how do you develop some confidence in yourself?

Let's start with something most people are generally afraid of; public speaking. Many people so fear public speaking that their heart starts to pound through the chest, their palms sweat and the nerves gather into a ball in the stomach – and all before they even get up to speak. At this stage, some self-confidence would be ideal, and you get it simply by trusting yourself.

Before you get up there, concentrate on trusting yourself. If you get nervous, remind yourself to trust your self more. If you feel you are not getting the responses you want, remind yourself that you need to trust yourself. Say it as many times as you need to, out loud or in your head. Use it as your mantra, 'I trust myself. Trusting myself is what brings confidence.'

It may sound too simple but the fact of the matter is that all confidence is, is having trust in yourself. You may think lack of confidence means you are afraid but it actually is about not trusting yourself, and think about this; if you met someone you didn't trust wouldn't you be scared of them or at least a little wary of them? Trusting yourself in the area you need more confidence in is going to be all you need to have that inner strength and confidence shine through.

People may or may not have confidence in all areas of their lives but when they do, it shows. Realize when you see a confident person, that this is an area of their life they trust themselves in. It helps to take them off the very high pedestals you have placed them on too or you may never feel you can measure up, or reach that level of confidence yourself.

The reason so many of us put people who have confidence up on high pedestals is because it is something we ourselves want to achieve. We think confidence is what we want, but it is actually being able to trust ourselves more.

Trusting yourself more also makes it possible for you to trust others more and openness comes. You will feel a sense of freedom, because not being able to trust yourself is like being restricted or trapped. Imagine always questioning if you are doing the right thing, always doubting, always resisting moving forward constantly being in knots over life and all because you can't trust yourself.

Awareness is the key to most things. Stay aware that you just need a little more trust in yourself and confidence will follow.

If you are already a very confident person, you may have gained more understanding and insight into why you are so confident. Then look at areas of your life where you lack confidence, understanding that you just lack trust in yourself in that area.

They say being shy is a lack of confidence, but like confidence I think it has been misunderstood. Being shy is not a weakness or being afraid for most people. I don't see shy people that way at all. In a household with several children for example, every child has a way of getting energy. The shy child uses shyness to draw attention to themselves. That is how that particular child has learnt to survive.

This shyness behaviour may accompany the child into adulthood because it has worked for them in the past; 'if it isn't broke, why fix it?'. If the child has outgrown their shyness though, it is because they have found other ways to get energy, though they may still from time to time fall back on this old behaviour. The sub-conscious forgets nothing so they will always have this security.

Watch a shy person and see how much attention actually goes to them. Focus on a shy person and they receive your energy like a silent predator. People are conscious of a shy person in the group; wondering what they may be thinking. They may feel a need to drag them into conversations to help them come out of their shell more. Others may feel a need to protect them. The shy person receives energy from every such situation.

Once you get to know a person who has been dubbed shy you will soon see they are usually very strong individuals underneath who just don't find a need to talk as much as the rest. Get a shy person onto a subject they consider valuable to talk about and you may also be surprised at the amount of confidence they have in the areas they are conversant with.

Shy people are usually very comfortable with themselves. Not feeling a need to participate in senseless gossip or to conform to the social order of conversation, the shy person may be taking in the conversation around them and reading people. So many people feel when they go out that they have to talk to be included in the conversation.

The label of being shy is often seen as a weakness – that the shy person is frightened – but now I am sure you will never look at a shy person quite the same way again. Understanding others leads you to your answers and to deeper compassion for others. As far as your own confidence goes, work on trusting yourself in those areas you need to and just feel the positive energy flowing out and back as your trust grows, and so will your confidence.

The Put Down

The constant self-put-downs one inflicts on themselves on a daily basis is simply amazing. So many people judge themselves in a negative way time and time again.

They cook a meal that goes wrong; they call themselves idiots. They forget something – nothing major but they forget all the same – and they put themselves down again; call themselves stupid or something equally naughty.

They are insulting themselves daily. You can't stop them. It is like watching a car speeding too fast down a hill. You know they are going to spin out of control and crash, yet there is nothing you can do about it. When you become aware of how much you or a friend puts himself or herself down you may be shocked. So many people are not aware that they actually do it, that it has become an automatic, life-long habit; a very scary thought, but true.

When you are stuck for something to say, put yourself down to fill in time. When all else fails put yourself down. Get stuck on a set of instructions; put yourself down. Don't know how to play a game; run yourself down some more. Run into an obstacle or feel overwhelmed again; just run yourself into the ground. Make a joke at your own expense; still a form of put-down. Are any of these things so bad you would insult or abuse another person who did them? Of course not! So why assault yourself verbally? It is just a habit most people have nowadays. Especially don't fall into the habit of doing putting yourself down because the people around you are, and you think it's going to make you more socially acceptable in their eyes if you do what they do.

With each insult, with each verbal attack on yourself and with each put-down you are creating and accumulating negative energy that will come back so hard you won't even notice it until it is right on top of you. Energy has a way it seems of creeping up on you; it doesn't really but it can seem that way.

This self-putting-down comes in many forms. There are people who build others up by putting themselves down. For others the need to be accepted, to have people like and approve of them is so important that they willingly put themselves down to accomplish that. Others apologize for everything they do. They may have done nothing wrong but they apologize anyway, often simultaneously building others up so that they are accepted.

People who feel this constant need to apologize may have been in an abusive situation, or been abused as children so to avoid being hurt they constantly say they are sorry. It is a survival technique that they may have found difficult to let go of. Next time you hear someone saying sorry all the time and needing to constantly have to apologize, understand why and this will lead to compassion.

Putting yourself down is not going to bring you close to your goals or to the success you think you want to achieve in this life time. In fact you have more chance of blocking that success. By putting yourself down you create much negative energy coming back to you and only a very tiny amount of positive energy. How much positive energy do you put out daily? How many times daily do you put yourself down? If the positive energy is five steps forward how many steps back does the negative energy take you? You may want to be more aware of how much you put yourself down in a day. You can get friends and family to keep an ear out for you doing it and to pull you up about it. It really does help. Plus it may actually help your loved ones in the process.

Thinking in terms of putting others down, do you engage in idle gossip during the day? Gossip is a way of bonding, but it is also a way of bullying other people. It can't make someone feel good when you are constantly running them down now can it? Verbal and mental abuse is just as bad as the physical kind. The energy that can come off a group of women or men in the throws' of putting someone down is enough to hurt anyone who is such a target.

Now here is what will really bite. When you put another person down or judge them in any kind of a negative way, what you are saying is actually how you feel about yourself. Life is a reflection of us. Life is reflecting back to us daily. If you pay someone a compliment that is how you feel about yourself. When you put someone down it is how you really feel about yourself inside.

Suppose you lack confidence in an area of your life. You may be ashamed of that but it seems hidden until you judge another person on it; maybe putting them down for being so shy and suggesting they should join in more. It is actually how you feel about yourself.

Consider a person who looks attractive and seems to take pride in themselves, yet if you listen to them talk you may find that they see an overweight person and run themselves down. You may be surprised, but this indicates that they actually don't feel as secure about their weight as you thought they did.

I find some people who work out and look amazing, are doing it for the wrong reasons; to suppress emotions and feelings that are in the too hard basket for them. They measure themselves on how good they look or where their body fat is. Others work out to hide their insecurities and they need to deal with them as well or their bodies will give out in some way; perhaps they will find at one stage or another the weight will come back on and they may find it more difficult to take it off yet again.

Next time you even think of putting someone else down, take time to reflect. What are you perhaps saying about yourself? Next time you hear a person putting another down, you know it is how they feel about themselves. You will realize that you have reached a new level of awareness. Understanding is everything and awareness is key.

Venting

Many of us, if not all of us have vented at one time or another to release some form of emotion or feeling that has built up or been suppressed through out the day or even longer. We all need to vent occasionally but you are still responsible for the energy you put out as that energy will return to you.

To vent is your choice and always has been; nothing has changed there. But consider this; if you were actually paying attention or being aware of how you were feeling and were dealing with emotions as they arose, then there would be no need to vent.

Here's an example that may help you start looking at venting with a different view and then you may start trying to understand exactly why you are venting in the first place.

A wife who stays home and cleans the house each day gets little appreciation for it though she finds it very exhausting, and suffers from ill health and pain daily.

One day the washing machine floods the house. She has no one to talk to so she may suppress her anger.

Her husband comes home from work and he does one small thing that she has mentioned before that annoys her. She vents all those emotions that she has been feeling all day by yelling at him.

The wife may say, 'I don't like yelling at you but you should just listen.' But she has not been completely honest because she really does enjoy venting by yelling at her husband, otherwise she would find another way to communicate. Her pay off from venting through yelling at her husband is to release all that built up emotion.

Many of us choose to vent as a way to avoid talking about their true feelings; a way of never having to deal rationally with their situation, emotions and feelings. Next time you want to vent take a moment to check in with yourself and ask why you feel this strong need to do so. Ask what you are trying to mask or not deal with. You might be surprised by your answer.

By taking a little time out to understand yourself you will find that you can take back more of your control. Venting is just expressing without thinking about it. If you are wondering why things are not going right for you in your life you may want to take a moment and really hear yourself when you are venting because when you vent negativity you get negativity back in return.

Expectations

I have spoken about expectations incidentally throughout the pages of *Who Stole My Energy?*. But to make their role crystal clear for you, I thought they deserved their own section.

An expectation is a thought about a future outcome, which you then draw in. If you regularly have expectations that are not realized, the reason for that is very simple; you were not expecting what you may have thought. This comes from lack of awareness of your own thoughts, words and actions. You may truly believe you know what you are thinking but are you truly aware of every thought you are having? If you are aware of each and every thought you are having then you would have everything that you have expected to come into your life.

Your thoughts are energy just as your words and actions are, each of these being your thoughts, words and actions can form your expectations or can create your expectations. What energy in the form of your expectations you put out creates and manifests your reality and the life you find yourself living in today.

You may have an expectation of how your life should be, but then you may have a small doubt about this and you think it may be a small doubt because you suppress this doubt, and so out of sight, out of mind, so to speak. This small doubt has blocked what you wish to create in your life. What your expectations may have been has been blocked by you not being aware of all your thoughts and feelings and words and actions.

If you expect to be successful in a business venture or even a job interview, your expectation is that of success and a good outcome for you. But you say with your mind and thoughts that you are nervous about your job interview and there is your block to receiving your success, that one thought of being nervous is going to sabotage your successful result.

We have so many expectations about how things will be, and how life should be for each and every one of us. Expectations are creating your reality and your life you are living today. How you expect your life to turn out is going to exactly go as you expect, if you are aware of your thoughts, words and actions.

It must seem like it would be a lot of hard work to be aware of your thoughts, words and actions all the time, but if you were you would be in more control of you and your life and manifest more of what you want and need, instead of the complete opposite.

To help manifest your expectations of how you want your life to be, and take back your control, see it not as hard work but more for your benefit. Take brushing your teeth – it is something most of us do everyday. We learnt when we were younger how to brush our teeth and at first it may have felt like a chore but now it is something we do without even thinking about it much. So to will being aware of your expectations.

What you expect of yourself you create and draw into your life. What you expect of others and how you may even expect them to react you also create and manifest and draw into your life.

What do you expect to happen next in your life? What do you expect is just around the corner for you? What are your expectations for your business, your relationships or your health? Whatever your expectations may be they are a very powerful way to manifest and create a reality that you may find yourself living in today.

Next time you expect someone to be late, ask yourself why you wanted that. As do realize that with each expectation you are asking for and/or requesting that to happen, or for that energy to be drawn into your life.

Expectations if you are aware of them more, you can make them work for you and not against you, and the only way an expectation can work against you is if you are not aware of what you are expecting through your mind and thoughts, words and actions.

Your expectations are very powerful tools to help you draw in what you want. Expect the negative or the worst in a situation and manifest that, or you could choose to expect the positive and a beneficial outcome and create something that helps you instead of hindering you.

Your expectations are a tool to help you, and it is up to you to utilize them or not. This is your choice as this is all about getting to know you, the more you know about yourself the better equipped you are in helping yourself create a life you want and need, instead of something you may have thought once you just had to put up with.

Judgment

I have spoken about judgment throughout these pages as something we are constantly doing. We just can't seem to help ourselves. People just judge themselves and one another; in good ways and bad. Judging others is a habit many of us will never grow out of, but it is something that we can strive to learn from.

The constant need to judge is an untapped opportunity to learn, grow and elevate. We are our own teachers and gurus and judgment is one of our greatest sources of teaching material, from which to teach yourself about healthy and unhealthy habits and behaviours and about you. We have so much to learn from ourselves first.

Without perhaps even noticing it you also teach others every day because there is always someone around watching you, who holds you in high regard. So you are leading by example without even wanting to. Everyone has something to teach; often people have a wealth of knowledge and do not even realize it. Something you take for granted could often help so many others.

The act of judging another person involves seeing that positive attribute or negative fault in yourself. So when you judge another that is how you see yourself on some level. When you hear a person judge another, that is how they feel about themselves in some way and on some level. When you judge another in a negative way you show your insecurities to everyone around you. It is like putting your private thoughts out there for the whole world to see. Realize, when you judge another, that they may have read these pages and that you have just shared your insecurities with them, by judging them in a negative way.

It may seem unreal to think that a person who appears to have their life together and be healthy, strong, fit and beautiful would ever see themselves as fat or overweight. But when they put down a person who is not thin then they show that they are still not happy or confident with the body they have.

This also goes for people who engage in gossiping, or bullying another person. Backbiting and back-stabbing are just judgments presented in a different form and as such, show the world the insecurities of the backbiter or back-stabber.

I believe judgments are also a cry for help that many of us don't hear. We have been taught to believe that when another judges you in a bad way you should accept their judgment and perhaps even react badly or take it in a bad way, instead of trying to understand the deliverer of the judgment and their situation. They may not want your help, but at least why they are judging is exposed along with their feelings, vulnerabilities and insecurities.

This does not give people who gossip or bully license to pick on others, but makes you aware that putting down another person with negative judgments actually shows the insecurities of the deliverer to everyone and anyone.

People can talk themselves into almost anything. Children, for example, talk themselves into being sick. They walk around saying, 'I feel sick,' and they continue until they get sick. Some bring this into adulthood too. People do exactly the same with gossip. They talk themselves into not liking someone just by talking about a person in a negative way. Judging someone creates an expectation of that person and you end up drawing that in. But why talk yourself into judging someone badly? Gossiping is a lazy way of bonding. We all want to fit in and belonging to a gossiping group gives so many of us the chance to fit in, to make friends and to feel as though we belong.

But this kind of negative gossiping is abuse; plain and simple, and if you put out the energy of abusing another, you get it back. When you judge another in a negative way, it draws energy in. You draw in negative energy, because you have hurt another, and you hurt yourself, because judging another is also how you feel about yourself so you are also putting yourself down.

The solution is pretty easy. First you need to take the time to understand yourself and to un-clutter your mind, so you can regain your balance and control over your life. Then just be a little nicer and kinder to yourself. This will filter through to all areas of your life. If you see yourself in a constructive and positive way you can't possibly judge another in a negative way. This is an ongoing transformation, so don't be too hard on yourself as you will have to undo years of programming.

Then, when you see someone, tell them they are looking stunning, beautiful, amazingly gorgeous or whatever positive trait you may see in them. That is then how you start to feel about yourself and/or you start to see and focus more on your positive traits instead of your negative ones. Whatever you focus on grows, so you can either focus on the negative traits and draw that energy into your life, or you can focus on the positive traits and draw that energy instead. You may focus your thoughts at times on how overweight you are or how unfortunate you are in your looks or any other negative trait, but if you start to see the beauty and the more positive in another person, then you may find that is who you really are inside. The more you focus on the positive traits the more they can magnify and manifest in your life. Through seeing the beauty in other people, you will start to see just how beautiful you really are. Then you can allow yourself to be beautiful. True beauty comes from the inside out.

Some overweight people may hear from others that 'beauty starts from within'. The thing is it is really true. No one is going to feel absolutely and totally one hundred percent beautiful until they have worked on their inner selves. Healing your true self by knowing and understanding yourself better is going to give you the power to be beautiful and it will give you confidence as well. Remember that confidence is just trusting yourself and it's a beautiful, stunning, gorgeous quality that attracts other people.

Judging another reveals the secrets of your soul.

—Renee Henderson

When we judge another or even ourselves, it reveals everything about us. There are no secrets. When you think you are keeping yourself and everything about you a secret, realize it is not that much of a secret anymore once you judge yourself or others realize you have revealed your self to others.

This understanding of judging yourself and others may make you feel uncomfortable, to the point where you might be triggered to respond. It will take some getting used to. The only solution to deal with this triggered response is to embrace this new understanding. Then take the opportunity to learn more about yourself through the judgments you make of others and yourself. They are a chance to elevate, to bring clarity where there was none, seeing life a lot clearer and so being able to see your path and know where to walk; your life direction. Judgment of others and self is a great place to start your journey to clarity and growth.

Mind Talk

By your thoughts, by your beliefs, by your imagination, by your will, you create, guide, and maintain your life.

You are the creator of the movie of your life. Nothing happens by accident or chance, it is all cause and effect. If cause was sown during a past frame of your life-movie, when the effect comes along it is seen as either good or bad luck, chance, coincidences, or an accident. Time separates!

Despite appearances, life does not work in this manner. You shape and mould the life you live.

You create your fortune and misfortune.

It is a good idea to remember this, and apply it to your ongoing moment.

-Michael J. Roads. The Oracle

Our minds and our thoughts are energy and so our thoughts and this form of energy is put out and can also be returned to us. If we are aware of our thoughts and what energy we are putting out, we can then control what is returned to us and so manifest and create a life we want.

If you listen to your thoughts you will realize throughout the day there is a lot of chatter going on in your mind, lots of Mind Talk.

If you pay attention to this Mind Talk and what your mind and thoughts are telling you, then realize that this is what you choose to believe about yourself. You choose what you think, you choose your thoughts, you are in control of what you think.

When you begin to listen to the chatter you may find you hear similar conversations in your mind over and over again. Then if you are being aware of your thoughts you may hear what is creating your life to be a certain way, you may begin to understand why your health is not the best, or you do not have the personal or professional life you really wanted. Simply by paying attention to your Mind Talk you can help and even assist your own healing process and also gain the rewards you desire.

How do you do this? You become aware of your thoughts, realize what you think creates your reality you live in. You are in control of your thoughts and so you are in control of how your life will manifest. You are not your thoughts, because you are in control of them and you can choose what you want to think.

Each thought or conversation you have with yourself is maybe adding stress, tension or pressure, or your thoughts may be creating understanding, ease, improved health, less tension and a happier you. Your thoughts have that much control and power, and you are not your thoughts; you decide what you think and what thought you are going to have from moment to moment.

You may find when you hear your Mind Talk it is very busy, crowded, cluttered, confusing and there is so much havoc in your mind. If this is happening with your mind talk, then be sure that is what is in your life. Your life is a reflection of your thoughts.

There may be havoc in your life, lack of clarity and life direction. You may even feel lost in life, or even feel trapped. You may wonder why this is happening to you, or that you really don't deserve a life like you are presently living.

When you focus on a thought it magnifies and grows, so if you focus on a negative thought it magnifies and this could also be contributing to the havoc in your surroundings.

When you start to hear what your mind is chatting about, you take back your power. You take back your power to choose what you think and so realize you control your own Mind Talk and what energy you put and so what energy is drawn back into your life.

Ask yourself: What do I think about? What is my Mind Talk? Then look at your life and you will find those thoughts you have been having has created the life you are living in now.

Chapter 4   Resistance

Wisdom will only increase with

Attempts made to destroy.

-David Baird. A Thousand Paths to wisdom

When you change anything in your life, be it how you see yourself, your physical self, or even healing a long term health condition, you are more often than not going to resist with all your will.

Excuses, self-sabotage, obstacles created, blocks and doubting are all examples of natural resistance to change, at its best. Feeding into an emotion, complaining constantly and whining are all forms of resistance too.

Resistance makes trying to change yourself just like pushing on a door marked pull. Though you feel you want to change, nothing is moving forward. It can drive you crazy. You are resisting but are not aware that you are resisting, just can't see for looking and so nothing is moving in your life.

People resist feeling certain emotions for fear of feeling vulnerable or embarrassed. They may resort to any measures to resist feeling these emotions; they may even physically hurt themselves so they don't have to deal with anything for the time being.

Many people with long-standing, even painful health conditions that they may have had all their lives, get help and actually find it is starting to help them. They start to see an improvement and then they create resistance; they can't cross that finishing line to their new and better life. Getting well and healthy is taking them right out of their comfort zone. At the deepest level, they would actually prefer to stay ill because that is all they know; they know nothing else. Without their illness, they have lost their security and they feel vulnerable, fearful and it is a scary place for them to be. This fear creates stress, anxiety and a whole lot of emotions that can cause more blocks.

Eventually the illness returns to its status quo and they feel safe and secure again.

Their condition has been their talking point. It is their way of getting attention and energy; of interacting with others. They have done all their communicating around their illness or disease and don't know anything else. When they make a change in their life as big as healing a health condition it is like starting over; needing to learn to communicate all over again. People have to realize once they give up their resistance and choose to heal they are going to have to learn a new way to communicate with others.

Another reason people resist healing is that after many years of dis-ease, it is like being trapped in an abusive cycle in which they have been abused emotionally, mentally and physically. The ill health can dominate people, making them a slave, trapped inside their own body, seemingly forever. When someone else is helping them to heal, the expectation is for the person they are helping to walk away from their abusive relationship just like that. Many people who are in actual abusive relationships find it difficult to walk away and people with ill health or dis-ease find it just as difficult when they have to leave it behind. This can be another reason why so many resist a healing method that works for them.

Many people will continue to remain in an abusive relationship because that is all they know. The fear of change is scarier than having to put up with someone with whom they may be unhappy, but who they know because change is feared far more. When someone resists moving on from their abusive relationship or ill health just realize that as it is all they know and have known for so long, that it is difficult to walk away.

If you are in a situation where you are resisting healing a long-standing illness don't be too hard on yourself and don't beat up on yourself for not healing. Realize that there are many layers to deal with when walking away from an illness. When you beat up on yourself it is just another way of resisting. Think about it. When you beat up on yourself are you moving forward or backwards? Beating up on your self is pure abuse and just another way to avoid healing. You might think, so then what do I do? The solution is first, don't beat up on yourself, and second, realize you haven't failed. You only fail if you stop trying.

Resistance is a wonderful teacher no doubt about it. Much can be learnt from resistance, so much can be learnt even by observing someone who is resisting. It opens your eyes when you observe another person, and with understanding you gain wisdom and with this newfound wisdom you may be able to add to someone else's life. By observing I mean understanding someone, you not only elevate and grow from understanding, but so does anyone you pass this information along too. We are all here to elevate, which means to grow.

If you are not actively elevating and gaining growth when you are in a relationship with someone, you are not growing and so you will find the relationship will start to collapse. First small things will fracture and then they will get bigger and bigger until all hell breaks loose and it ends badly. When you stop elevating or growing together in a relationship and you don't try to correct that or leave then you are resisting change. If you don't you are moving against the current of life, which is pure resistance. There is no way around it – you must elevate.

If you are elevating in a particular area of life then you are not resisting in that area of life. If you meet someone and wonder if you have made a connection, see if they elevate you or not. If not, then move on. If you spend all your time elevating someone else or holding him or her up all the time and it is not mutual then it will drain you of energy. Staying with someone who is not elevating you constitutes resistance – you are resisting moving forward in your life.

In other areas of your life if, you stop from time to time and take stock, and realize that you are not moving forward ask yourself if you are actually resisting in any way at all; complaining, blaming, making excuses, avoiding things or people are just some of the forms of our resistance.

If you stop resisting you will begin to move forward more, the change you may have feared once begins to flow more in your life and so more opportunities start to flow into your life more.

Isn't it more helpful and constructive to have opportunities flowing into your life more than not. Take a moment and see where you are resisting in your life, is it in your professional life, your career, in your relationships, in your marriage, maybe with your health. Imagine being without resistance in one of these areas of your life. Imagine seeing the energy flow into these areas and imagine for a moment what opportunities could flow into these areas of your life, that can only help you to grow more, and if nothing else open new doors for you. Letting go of resistance is like closing one door so another door may open.

Complaining

All things are happy when are still.

When we fight in order to accomplish, we disturb
the gentle balance that exists.

Therefore, the wise man never

fights but remains still.

-Daniel Levin. The Zen Book

If you are constantly complaining, it is an indication that you can't be seeing the good that is going on around you or in your life. You must only be seeing the negative in everything, and that is being returned to you.

Complaining, whining or moaning and groaning are all ways to resist dealing with something or anything.

As long as you are moaning about something you are not actually dealing with it or repairing the situation.

If you moan and groan about your tooth hurting, that is not going to fix it. It may actually make it worse. There will be no improvement until you go and get some help physically. Like life, many people like to moan and groan but few do anything about improving their situation.

Think about the time one invests in complaining all the time. If you used that time in a constructive way like actually trying to understand why you haven't got this or that in your life – or the reason whatever you are complaining about is happening – you may actually be able to clear it and turn things around. An investment in complaining is an investment in resisting, not moving forward in your life.

When you see faults in others and complain about them, you judge another in a negative way, which, as we have said, is a reflection of who you really are. You can't find fault in another unless you hold the same or similar faults within you.

Also to find fault in another and complain about it is a way to resist dealing with your own faults. You may even be resisting something more and this complaining is just masking a much bigger problem.

When someone comes home from work and complains about their day, it may be a nice release. It still creates energy to go out and come back, but it may be a nice release all the same. If it becomes habit, however, then it probably indicates resisting something a little bigger than just how they are feeling. They may be resisting what is really bothering them or what they need to do but haven't yet had the courage to face up to.

You find people who complain endlessly about the same thing. They are just going in circles, which is a wonderful way to resist. If you are bleating away with complaints and thereby resisting, then nothing changes and you feel safe and secure. When you complain on and on it is a huge investment of energy and time considering you are running around in circles, so what are you getting back for those efforts?

Next time you complain, stop and ask yourself, 'What am I resisting? What is so difficult for me to face?' It could be that you do not have something or someone in your life that you need. If this is the case then think about it. All the energy you have been putting out with your complaining, whining, moans and groans is energy that is going to be returned to you. You get as good as you give out with energy. If you haven't got what you think you deserve in life, check in with yourself and see what you have complained about lately. The key to getting what you want is you – it is always you.

You may have been complaining for so many years that it is just one jumbled mess and you may no longer realize why you complain so much. If you are at this point it is because you are using complaining to hide bigger issues and resist so much, that you may have lost track.

The solution is to stop complaining and try understanding the situation. Is there something you don't want to face? If you get a feeling or an emotion, it could be you not wanting to get honest about something. You may even be complaining because it is something you know and it is just easier to do this. Whatever the reason, it is just you resisting and complaining gives you that exit out of any situation or experience you want to resist. It is your choice to resist, and it is your choice to complain.

Complaining is taking a situation and seeing an obstacle instead of an opportunity. You make this choice. See it as an obstacle and you stop yourself dead in your tracks. Your growth stops and you cease moving forward. See it as an opportunity to elevate and grow and you win along with everyone around you.

Seeing a situation as an opportunity instead of complaining about it does help others. If you complain, you draw in energy to reflect your complaining, but this energy also permeates you. This energy then goes onto infecting others around you, and they will become irritable toward you;

maybe even angry. This is because they are reacting to your negative energy.

When you complain about something you are judging in a negative way and when you judge another in a negative way you draw in the energy related. The energy returned as a result of your complaining or negative judgement is people gossiping about you, telling you lies, back-stabbing you or worse, verbal, emotional, mental and physical abuse.

Next time you want to complain about something or someone, think about it. Check in with yourself and see if it is healthy for you or unhealthy for you. Less resistance is going to make your life path a lot easier, a lot safer and a lot clearer. If you can't see your life path you are not going to see your life direction. You are going to be lost and wandering around in the darkness. If you have less resistance in your life then you are going to see your life path and be able to move forward a lot easier and with much more confidence.

Avoidance

Avoidance is a very familiar behaviour that many of us have at one time or another tried on; avoiding doing something or seeing someone for instance. It is all resistance. Why do so many of us want to complicate our lives with so much resistance? All of us have the choice to make about whether or not our lives will be easy or difficult. Resistance just makes life that little bit harder.

Resistance is not something you are likely to be able to give up over night. But the more aware you are of your resistance, the better the chance you have of making your life a little clearer and by clearer I mean less clutter, less confusion, more clarity and direction. The clearer you see your life, the more confident you can be about where you place that next step of yours.

Let's start with common avoidance like avoiding certain people in our lives; eg someone who can actually help you or who is presently helping you. Maybe it is a friend or family member who knows you so well that you can't pull the wool over their eyes, so you avoid them. You don't want to change. You don't want to hear the truth because the truth is so hard to bear, or it will mean you having to get honest with yourself and move forward.

As a result of trying to avoid these helpful people you will just put out a negative energy with your avoidance and so with your resistance, that in time comes back to you, in the form of others being dishonest with you or something similar. You may find people you like and maybe want to spend time with start to avoid you. Why? Because you give off energy that they are just not attracted to, seriously would you want to be friends with a dishonest person? Then you also draw in other energies like people being dishonest with you in return.

If avoidance fails then you may just be rude to the person and hurt their feelings. That is the next extreme step in avoidance, one I don't recommend.

You will certainly avoid and resist any lesson or chance to elevate that way and you won't have to move forward or change your life for the better. You may lose your friend in the process though. So is the pay off worth losing someone you care about for; someone that actually honestly cared about you? Next time you go to avoid someone who is trying to help you, you may want to take a moment to think about a healthier choice. The healthier the choice the healthier the energy coming back to you is. Make the energy work for you, not against you, to improve your life.

Dodging someone so you don't have to talk to him or her is avoidance and you have to ask yourself why you are really avoiding this person. Are they reflecting you and/or your insecurities? If you avoid someone because of something they said it might indicate there is an energy block that needs to be cleared. Ask yourself why you are avoiding them? What lesson could you be trying to learn and understand here to clear this?

To keep avoiding someone is going to drain you of energy, because to avoid someone you are giving your focus to that person and that is where your energy is going. As you have not dealt with the reason why you are avoiding that person, you are going to have all the anxiety and stress and worry over having to avoid someone, creating an energy block. This energy block will continue to feed energy to this person until you deal with the reason you are avoiding them – maybe for life! Not to mention the energy that flows back to you as a result of your initial avoidance.

Aloof behaviour is also an avoidance technique. Someone who is aloof is a predator for energy; it is the main way they know of to get energy. They have learnt it at a young age and it has stayed with them. When you ask someone who is aloof a question and they refrain from giving an answer and make you wait, that is classic predator behaviour.

When you talk to someone who is aloof and they look off in another direction and you have to go out of your way to bring their attention back to you so that you can talk, all that effort to get them to turn around and face you or give you some attention, goes to the aloof person.

Aloof people also often practise selective hearing and seeing, which allows them to avoid and resist as they want. If they don't want to deal with a problem or listen to someone else anymore they just use their aloof behaviour to avoid anything they don't want to hear. This is taking one of life's blessings and turning it into an obstacle instead of an opportunity to learn and grow.

If you are aloof, realize what you are doing when avoiding what someone is saying. You are getting energy, sure, and you will feel a rush for a very short time, but you will be hurting someone, causing pain and injury to someone emotionally. Remember that if that is the energy you are putting out, that pain will come back to you. No one is trying to punish you for being aloof. This is just the real price you will pay, that you ask for when you decide to be aloof. It is your choice.

Avoiding someone is resistance, but avoidance is also a lie.

Excuses

You make goals and you make promises. When you break them, you have an excuse so that makes it all right. You are pardoned. People often hide behind so many excuses that excuses become a crutch in their lives.

You promise yourself something that you don't follow through on, so you resort to old habits and make an excuse. You pardon yourself yet again. Yet these excuses are actually just a part of resistance to change.

How many people talk themselves out of going to the gym to work out or staying on a healthy diet? How many excuses do we employ to accomplish this? It is amazing how many excuses we can use to get ourselves out of something we don't want to do. We are just plain lying to ourselves when we make these excuses. We need to sit ourselves down and get honest with ourselves. Take it as an opportunity to elevate yourself. Ask yourself, okay why don't I really want to workout? Why don't I want to change my life? Why am I holding myself back?

Remember that in many endeavours that involve change and effort, the first thing you are likely to find yourself doing is making excuses. Excuse making is a life long habit you are trying to break, so it will not be easy but it is, at least, something that can be improved upon.

Instead of excuses, try honesty. Again, this does not give you licence to be rude or blunt to yourself or others. Being honest with yourself and others makes life a lot easier and less stressful. If you make a false excuse to get out of something and get caught, think about how much stress that causes as a result, whereas if you had just been honest you would be a lot lighter and a lot clearer. Simple really, but people want to make it difficult.

People find excuses for everything and anything, all to avoid something they don't really want to do. They would rather make an excuse, lying to both themselves and others than to be honest. Excuses and the associated lies we tell ourselves and others daily are the foundation our lives are resting on. As such, they make for a very weak life foundation; one that cannot take too many knocks. Strengthen your life foundation by stopping yourself next time you feel a need to make an excuse, and asking yourself why you are making excuses instead of being honest with yourself and others. Then that is at least a start to moving in the right direction and strengthening your life foundation.

I find people can be really mean to themselves. I see people with health conditions that are created by their emotions and being mean to themselves. The solution is to be a little nicer to yourself, a little kinder and honest with yourself, saving yourself a lot of pain and unnecessary suffering.

Making excuses is not taking responsibility for who you are and not respecting yourself enough to say I want this but I don't want this for now or forever. Take back your power by being honest with yourself, taking responsibility and making an effort to nurture yourself.

Blame

Reduce your need to blame.

Increase your ability to appreciate.

Seems simple enough! Yet, people mostly go into 'automatic blame' at the slightest incursion upon their perceived rights.

This indicates that people who blame others automatically, also automatically blame themselves.

In other words, while you have a critical self-blame relationship with yourself, this negative cycle will continue.

Again, it begins with you and yourself.

When you find the way to appreciate yourself instinctively, you will instinctively appreciate the other people in your life.

As always, this attracts even more people and situations to appreciate.

-Michael J. Roads. The Oracle

Blame is a favourite form of resistance used by so many who find someone or something to blame instead of taking responsibility. We even make jokes about it; the dog ate my homework!

We use blame as our scapegoat so many times, to get out of so much as at the time it seems to lighten your burden. When you blame someone it takes the responsibility off your shoulders and places it on someone else. You may even actually convince yourself the person you blamed is truly at fault – you probably do.

Take a health condition for instance. After being ill for a long time and not getting well, you believe that it can't be your fault so you look for someone to blame. Normally that is the person who is helping you. By blaming the person who is helping us we are giving away our power. The more power you give away the worse your condition may become. So what can you do instead? As a couple of examples, you may want to look at how negative you have been during your condition, how emotional you have been and whether you tried to learn from these emotions or fed into them. Changing your state of mind and how you deal with your emotions can have a huge impact on some health conditions.

After a minor car accident, in many cases the drivers will jump out of their vehicles and start blaming one another or something external, instead of taking responsibility themselves. Remember I mentioned earlier that a car accident may be caused by someone putting out negative energy through judging themselves or another in a negative way. This negative energy accumulates and comes back. One way the energy can be returned to you is packaged as a car accident. All energy is returned – today, tomorrow or whenever. It will come back.

When something good happens to us we take credit for it straight away. We get a job promotion or a pay rise and we say, 'I deserved that! I worked hard for that.' We can't wait to take credit for it. But when we lose a job, we look for someone or something to blame. It can't be our fault. Someone must have done something – but no way could it ever be your fault. Such an experience can then take you right off balance.

You give your power away when you blame another person for anything that happens in your life. As soon as you give your personal power away you lose balance. Then you lose focus. The next minute life can seem to be filled with obstacles and it takes time to realign yourself with your path.

Let's look at what can be learnt from the job loss situation. Ask yourself, 'What energy did I put out to create this?' Consider whether you could have exuded an energy that indicated that you felt that you could do better than this job, or that you wished you didn't have to work anymore, or that you hated the job and your work colleagues were fools. In such cases, the energy is just giving you what you asked for. It is that self talk again, that unseen language. If you don't keep an eye on it, it will sneak up behind you and bite you so hard that it will knock you off balance.

Blaming others for situations instead of taking responsibility is giving up and throwing away your power and control, leaving you and your life foundation unsupported and weakened. With no strength in your foundation, and unaware of an energy you have put out, it comes back and you will take a knock from which it can take a long time to recover.

When we were children we were very quick to blame one another so we wouldn't get in trouble. We learnt at such a young age, that if you blame someone first, even though you did it, you would not get in trouble or punished and there was a real possibility you would get away with it. And if you were the innocent one getting blamed all the time and getting punished, you still learnt this behaviour. Either way, blaming is learnt behaviour.

Then it becomes like a knee jerk reaction. Something goes wrong, something breaks, and you look for someone else to blame because you might actually get away with it. You can say 'See it is not my fault that I am this way', but we all know right from wrong. When you feel this overwhelming need to blame someone or something else, please ask yourself what you are resisting and why. Once you have gained some awareness and understanding of the situation you will be able to clear it a lot faster and you will have stopped giving that all important energy and power away.

Past

Many of us hang onto the past; some of us even still live in the past. Living in the past is resisting the present and the future.

It is important to know about someone's past, especially if you are entering a new relationship and it is nice to share past experience's. But when your new partner wants to know about the ex-boyfriend or ex-husband or ex-girlfriend or ex-wife (or vice versa), this is where the problems start.

Assuming, for example, that in finding out about your partner's ex, you discover the fact that they were divorced because your partner had an affair. This is going to cause you problems in your present relationship. So the past is going to rob you of your future.

You may say the past affair doesn't worry you but it will. The subconscious will store every memory ready to rear its ugly head later. You go out with your partner one evening and your partner looks at no one in particular, but in you pounce. The green-eyed monster of jealousy makes its presence felt and you become possessive, suspicious; and it may not even be like you. This is that memory you stored coming to the fore, and the past destroying the future for you.

The thing is, many of us know that talking about the past and about someone you had strong feelings for is not really benefiting anyone so why do it? You can't change what happened in the past. Take the opportunity to learn what is of importance from it, clear what you need to and let it go. And leave the rest to lie.

If you let your past continue to dominate your present life it will dictate your future as well. Many people give their power away to their past. Some bury their past and don't deal with it though they still have related energy blocks that they need to deal with and clear. Others openly live in the past but still don't clear it, or deal with it. They just run in circles, going over and over the same problems and issues and never getting anywhere.

Hanging onto your past like this is resisting your present life and your future. You deserve to move into a future full of life and not be dragged down by the past – which can't be changed. But many of us choose to live in the past because then we have something, a tool, to use to resist anything we don't want to deal with or face. We can blame our past for nothing going right in our lives. We can, for instance, say that what happened to us in the past is the reason why we are the way we are or not getting what we want out of life.

This is giving their power away to the past. Imagine that power is money and imagine every time you give your power away you are throwing money away. Then, maybe, just maybe you might give it some thought and be a little more aware.

We need to let go of anything that no longer serves us.
How long must we carry the burden of the past?

Don't be a slave to your past. Don't use your past as resistance not to get on with the rest of your life. You are in control of this life; no one else. It is a matter of using just a little more understanding to clear your past and then it will not be your master and you won't be its slave any more.

Beliefs

Your beliefs shape the way you think, and your thoughts shape your beliefs.

It makes you wonder which came first!

Obviously thoughts have to precede our beliefs, to give them shape and meaning, yet it is those beliefs that then shape the way we think.

This is not necessarily a good cycle to get locked into. Once we have constructed a strong belief, we have created a box that will contain and limit our thinking. Let go of the need for beliefs, or, if this is not possible for you, release your attachment to the belief.

Non-attachment is one of the major requirements to be practiced along the path of spiritual Enlightenment.

—Michael J. Roads, The Oracle.

We all have our beliefs and to each of us, those beliefs are personal. I have my beliefs and I have written them down in the form of this book. They are what I live and breathe and strive everyday to achieve and maintain as they bring so much balance and calm into my life and into the lives of those I've shared them with. But they are one person's (my) beliefs. They are to give you insights, knowledge and tools for your everyday use; nothing more. I believe that everyone should learn as much as they can for themselves and create their own beliefs from what they have learnt and gained.

I have helped many people over the years, bringing about healing for them. Many of the cases in this book are experiences from people I have helped first hand to overcome obstacles in life. So when I talk about them it is from firsthand experience.

I have met people who have had a few curve balls thrown at them in this lifetime which have hit them hard and left their mark. As they say, 'What doesn't kill you makes you stronger' and I have seen this in many of the people who have come to see me. But you need to know that in life a little rain must fall sometimes for life to grow.

I helped many people to take back their power with just two simple tools; awareness and understanding. Seeing the results strengthened the beliefs that I share with you here in these pages.

Awareness branches in a thousand directions. Keeping every channel open is valuable.

These beliefs about understanding and awareness, that created *Who Stole My Energy?* are simple tools to which everyone has access. You too can gain help and healing with these two tools. Be prepared to open your mind and your heart, to see more clearly and to gain create your very own, or strengthen your own personal beliefs.

Some people try to put down the beliefs of others; some try very hard to do so. Fear too, can chase away one's beliefs and opportunities to grow and evolve.

I absolutely love what my beliefs do for me and I enjoy what they give me. With my beliefs I strive to learn more and push the boundaries, but many beliefs of today have boundaries and they give people security, and a nice safe and warm comfort zone. Beliefs make many feel safe in this very large world and universe.

Think about someone going to an unknown land, one that has never had anyone set foot on it before. This land would be all very new, unknown territory and it would all seem a little scary. But they take their beliefs about the world with them and so they have boundaries, they feel safe to step out into this new place, knowing that any obstacle can be overcome. Moving further inland in this new world is not so scary because they have their beliefs and boundaries to keep them safe and so they hold them dear. They hit obstacles and they fall back on their beliefs to give them the strength and understanding necessary to get them over these obstacles and keep them moving forward and feeling safe in the process. This is why so many hold onto their beliefs, because every day there is change in which one has to move out of their comfort zone. It is a lot easier to do so with your beliefs at your side. There is very good reason for holding onto beliefs, and a very good reason why people hang on so tightly to theirs. Their beliefs are their comfort zones and many would like to remain in their comfort zone and hide there, but that is their choice, and so their belief.

A great teacher once said: "It is easy to believe when thousands of people follow the same beliefs, but would we have the courage to believe if we woke up tomorrow and everyone believed differently?"

This is true belief – to believe what we do because it is really what we believe.

— Daniel Levin, The Zen Book.

Many people use their beliefs as a crutch, as resistance to avoid having to learn or grow. They use their beliefs to hide behind so they do not have to move out of their comfort zones. Their beliefs become that safe guardian to hide away in from having to take on other beliefs, and other truths that may rock their foundations by punching holes in their existing beliefs.

Then you have people who may be afraid of their world crumbling as a result of their beliefs being challenged. They may see some truth in someone else's beliefs but this only makes them more afraid and they become truly fearful. They prefer to use their existing beliefs, to stop having to face the challenges of growing and evolving. Some may use their beliefs as a safe haven to keep them nice and warm and secure in their comfort zones. There is nothing wrong with remaining in your comfort zone, and so remain in this comfort zone and get what you have always got, this is your choice, or make the change and challenge your beliefs and what you believe to be true, to gain growth and further understanding which can benefit you.

. . . If you have a concept of Truth, then live the concept. Either it will take you to the portal of Truth, or it will reveal to you that the concept was based in

We are all here to learn and grow, to elevate ourselves and to help others elevate. Instead of putting down someone else's beliefs if we listened to them we could heal and so could they. It would bring down the walls and boundaries. But so many people are afraid of the challenges of change that they hurt others from behind their own beliefs and run down anyone with different ones.

We have beliefs to keep us safe, we have beliefs to give us boundaries so we feel secure, and to help us to explain each new thing that comes along, from the basis of past experiences. But holding too tightly to beliefs becomes resistance to learning and developing spiritually, mentally, emotionally and even physically. Humans have evolved over millions of years by changing beliefs about how things are – albeit slowly at times – and we would do well to remember that. Stop resisting beliefs so that man and woman alike can continue to evolve. Our beliefs are only guidelines and do not give us license to hurt others.

Consider opening your heart to all beliefs and taking the time to learn about them as you are given the opportunity. You will grow and with time you will evolve your own beliefs; possibly create new ones. Either way they will be right for you at that time, but remember to keep your heart open to everyone and all beliefs and not to resist. Less resistance in life means fewer hardships. Allow yourself to evolve. Let go of your resistance so you can move forward, elevate and grow.

I would like to leave you with something to think about which I share from a book called *The Hidden Messages in Water* by the author Dr. Masaru Emoto.

And I have found the most beautiful crystal of all – the one created by 'love and gratitude.' This is supposedly what all the world religions are founded on, and if that were true, there would be no need for laws. You already know the answer. 'Love and gratitude' are the words that must serve as the guide for the world.

Chapter 5   Self Transformation

Self-Transformation is going to take you through some common areas of our lives we face every day, like going through *change* and the process our emotions go through and how to cope with this with better understanding of self.

Then you may want to change and yet you have no direction in life, or don't know what to do next in life and so are looking for an answer to help you find your direction and that is what *Reflections* is all about.

Then we move onto other areas of our life like finances or wealth, relationships be them in your personal or professional life and then of course your health. Each section will give you just a little more understanding into your emotions and energy and how they are either helping you or hindering your growth in these areas.

Also I thought is would be a good idea to add in a section on *Weight Management.* As I have seen and found from gaining an understanding into your energy, emotional behaviour and human behaviour and using these understandings within these pages of this book, that you not only take back control of your life but a side effect if you will, is weight loss. Many in this day and age struggle to get their weight off or to maintain their body weight, learn that if you have more understanding into you and your energy you will be making weight loss or maintaining your weight loss just a little more easier for yourself.

This section on Self-Transformation is about helping you gain further understanding into yourself and areas of your life that you may feel you need more understanding in.

Change

You cannot change and remain the same.

In my experience, just about everyone I meet wants to change and remain the same. Although generally unaware of it, those people who do want change cling to their destructive habits with incredible tenacity.

We invite change into our lives, and then fight either to remove it, or to avoid it.

Change is the fresh wind of new potential and new opportunities. It is not out to destroy you.

Change, will however, destroy all that is no longer appropriate in your life.

You have to learn to release it! It is far less painful to let change work with you, rather than against you.

— Michael J. Roads, The Oracle.

Change is just life's way of pruning back what it needs so you can receive a better harvest. Change is happening every moment of every day, though many people fear it. But everything is changing; always. You are at all times either moving forward or you are moving backwards. There is no standing still. You are forever in motion.

If you understand change is happening every second of every day, then it may help you to make changes in your life without fear.

The fact that change is always happening does not mean you cannot grieve for what could have been or what was. As change occurs in our lives, we have to deal with an array of emotions as we grieve for what once was but is no more. Allow yourself to grieve because by doing this you let go of the past and move into the future.

Many of us may see grief as a process we go through when someone passes away, but it also is a process we should allow ourselves with each new change in our life. If we end a relationship that is the end of one chapter in our life and we move into another. When we leave a job we have been in for years, a chapter in life has ended and another one must begin. But to get to that new chapter we need to grieve for the person that was as the new person emerges, otherwise the transition into the new chapter of our life may not go as smoothly as we may wish.

For example, many people lose weight and then gain it back. As the weight comes off they change as a person. Everything about someone who loses weight changes: size, appearance and outlook may change. Even one's personality can change. The overweight person begins to change with each pound that goes. Slowly over time they lose the person they once were but they may feel vulnerable or uncomfortable in this new person. They may not even be consciously aware of how uncomfortable it all feels. Maybe subconsciously the change has come too fast and they have not had a chance to grieve during the process so all their insecurities come out, without their conscious understanding of what is happening. This can lead to them regaining the weight, because losing it seems just too scary, and leaves them feeling too vulnerable and uncomfortable as they do not understand what they are feeling or what is coming up for them.

What they need to do, is to allow themselves, with each pound they lose, to grieve for the person they were, say goodbye and find a way to farewell that person. If they do this, it may allow them to never regain the weight again.

Just like everyone else, you are changing and evolving so you are always moving forward. Take the time to grieve for the person you once were and let that person go gently. Say a farewell. Then the new person has a much stronger foundation to stand on. You will feel more balanced and centered and from that point you will find that things cannot knock you as much as they may otherwise have done.

The most meaningful thing you can live for is to reach your full potential.

Many of us want to change direction in life or at least find our meaningful direction so we know which way to head. It seems to be such a huge obstacle to find your direction in this lifetime and to be a hundred percent sure you are on the right path.

The solution to finding your life path, to finding your life direction is to first understand yourself. Taking what is here in *Who Stole My Energy?* is as good a place to start as any. You may think that it might be too much effort to try to understand yourself but how much time have you invested so far trying to find your path, or being constantly worried you are not going anywhere in particular.

You may think you understand yourself just fine. If that is the case then *Who Stole My Energy?* should just confirm what you already know. If you feel you understand yourself then you should see your path and know exactly where you are going, exactly what needs to be done and have no worries about life direction. If this is the case for you, congratulations!

Finding your path is as easy as getting to know who you are, understanding who you are, being aware that every emotion has a job to do and letting your emotions do their job instead of feeding into them. It is also being totally aware at all times of your thoughts, words and actions. Once you have gained this awareness you will find it becomes second nature.

If the solution is so simple why haven't more people done this? Most of us believe consciously and subconsciously that any success that comes our way has to come from hard work. With such sayings as; "Success is sweet, but it usually has the scent of sweat about it." (Anonymous), it is no wonder so many of us have talked ourselves into believing that life has to be hard work and to achieve success this must mean you have to sweat blood. But in truth, achieving success in life is not about working harder but working smarter and *Who Stole My Energy?* is offering you one system by which to do this.

There are many systems out there and they all have something to teach. The more knowledge and insight you gain, the more tools you are going to have at your fingertips to help yourself and others with. Think of

Who Stole My Energy? as an opportunity to gain more understanding to help bring about change and to assist you in finding your direction.

Life may seem unfair sometimes and it may often seem that life has not come with an instruction manual. But life has given you the basic tools to get through this life. And to make that learning journey a little easier, two of these tools are *understanding* and *awareness*. You need the right tools for any job; you don't turn up to a building site with an eggbeater. As in life, you need the right tools for the job to make the job a little easier if you want to get through it. And life has given you tools; you just need to know how to use them. Use the tools of *understanding* and *awareness* to improve and refurbish yourself and your life through positive changes.

Reflections

Two dogs walk into a room.

One comes out quivering, barking in fear the whole time, while the other comes out wagging his tail, with a seemingly big smile across his face. A man seeing this walks into the room to discover that its full of mirrors. That is the way of this life: What we see is who we are.

— Daniel Levin, The Zen Book.

I have had many people ask me what should they be doing right now? We are talking about life direction, finding their path, or trying to even decide what line of business they should be in. So they are seeking a little direction in life. It is okay to want to change but then which way do they go? So I then ask them who do they spend time with? What do their friends and family do for a career? What do their friends and family have in common? As you read on you will find why I ask these questions.

The people, be they friends or family are reflecting back to you what you should be doing with your life. You could find you are surrounded by people who all own their own business of some sort. It is looking for the common reflection from everyone.

How you judge another is how you see yourself. How another judges you is how they see themselves. It is all just a reflection of one another. Your friends and family who you spend time with can even reflect back to you, what may be blocking you from succeeding in life. Take a look at the people you spend time with and you may see what is stopping them from achieving a goal and then look at your own life and see the reflection. It seems too easy to think that all your answers are right in front of you being reflected back to you, but they are.

Instead of going externally to find out what is blocking you from achieving your goals, first check in with yourself. Look around at the people you spend time with and amongst these people see what they are reflecting back and there lie your answers.

When you hear another judging a friend you spend time with, I suggest you pay special attention to what they are saying because this friend is someone you spend time with. This friend is a reflection of you. You may think I am nothing like that person, I ask that you take another look, a closer look and see if you really are like your friend even in a small way. We are just a reflection and everything and everyone is reflecting back to us the answers we need to help ourselves achieve our goals and success in life.

Everyone and everything around us is your teacher.

Ken Keyes Jr.

Handbook to Higher Consciousness

How can what your friends and family are reflecting back to you, help you? If you are trying to achieve successful weight loss and it has been difficult, look around at the people you spend time with. Are they overweight? Why do they eat? If you have friends around you who are attractive but still see themselves as unfortunate looking, why is that? If your friends are not overweight they may use their work or socializing, cigarettes, retail therapy, alcohol etc. to suppress, so why do they feel the need to suppress? Look at all their behaviours and see the reflections being reflected back to you. This will give you a good place to start, and that is one of many things your friends and family are reflecting back to you.

Have you ever looked for something and it was staring you straight in the face? Many answers you may be seeking are staring you right in the face every day.

If you allow yourself to see the reflections you will find your answers. Reflecting back to you is what is holding you back or blocking you from moving forward toward you achieving your goals. Life is filled with signs and signposts showing you the path to take and giving you answers to achieving your goals, it is up to you if you read them. It is your choice.

Life is just a reflection. It is that simple. Life isn't hard people make it that way. So let's work smarter not harder. Once you let life work for you things in life will begin to flow to you not around you.

Look for the reflections and take note and see what is reflecting back, by doing this you take another step closer to your personal success and gaining what you want as in your goals.

Allow yourself to become a magnet for success to come into your life. And it is as simple as opening your eyes and looking around at the people you spend time with. Here is another tool to assist you in achieving your own personal success and goals in your life.

Wealth

If one desires a change, one must be that change
before that change can take place.

—Gita Bellin

Here is a brief look at the subject of money and wealth, and an opportunity to understand another view of wealth. The more we understand about wealth and how we see it, the more chances there are of drawing more wealth into our lives. We can also find out what has been blocking wealth from coming into our lives.

Many of us look at money as a blessing. Some of us say, 'If only I had money' or 'If only I could win the lottery I would never have a problem again.' The thing is you can have all the money in the world but it will not buy you an escape from whatever is blocking your success, wealth, opportunity, happiness and/or relationship.

Some people who have money or who have a lot of wealth use it to resist life, opportunities and moving forward themselves. When a person receives wealth they not only receive money or material security; they also receive the many lessons that come with success. Many of the lessons that are given to someone with success and wealth can be very trying at times. If they find they have had enough of these lessons they may start to use up their money, wealth and success to suppress all the emotions and lessons that start to come up. In the process they can lose all of their wealth or a lot of it, though this can also be a lesson they can learn from.

To ask for wealth and money is to draw in more lessons to learn. You should first ask yourself whether you are able to deal with your present lessons; is your life foundation strong enough to take on more lessons. You need to be in position to be ready to receive wealth and maintain it.

Take the people you know who are rich or are celebrities, only to find out that they have substance abuse, broken marriages, eating disorders, and so forth. Money and fame don't exempt you from problems.

—Sylvia Browne, If You Could See What I See.

You may look at someone with money and think they are damn lucky, and that they don't have any problems. But try a little understanding to change the energy you put out to a healthier energy. What you see is a person with no money worries, but that is just one area of their lives. There is more to a person then just their wealth. They have just as many problems and life lessons as everyone else does.

Everyone has something they use to resist life with. When you have a lot of money you just have more to suppress with. I am not saying money is a bad thing – it makes this world go round – but I am trying to give you a different understanding of money so that you can see it from a different viewpoint, and change your attitude toward money. When you change your attitude toward money you change the energy. Realize money is just energy and so it is going to react to your energy.

What energy do you send out about wealth and money? Do you worry about money? The thing is when you worry about something like finances you tend to draw more of it in. Your energy doesn't judge you: it is your servant to do as you wish or instruct. If you worry about money, then your servant the energy, believes you would like more money worries and so that is what your energy gives you. Your energy has only done as you have instructed.

Do remember when you worry about something like wealth or your finances it doesn't change the outcome, so why worry about it.

If you worry about money, wealth and your finances you are blocking money from coming into your life. So if you go out now and worry about your finances or money or wealth then you are resisting wealth coming into your life. Ask yourself why you are doing that.

You have been playing the same song in your mind for a long time now, and if you continue to play the same song over and over again you will always get what you have always got, and nothing will change.

You may find you are standing still at the moment and just can't seem to push forward any further, or you may be someone who has financial problems, or you maybe just be doing okay but you want more. Then ask yourself what song you have playing; what energy have you been putting out toward money and wealth.

What song do you play yourself daily about your finances, money, wealth and/or success? Is this song drawing in what you want or is it blocking you?

When your desires don't come true, your awareness has suffered some block or disconnection from its source in the field. It is normal to have all desires be fulfilled if your awareness is open and clear.

Do you complain about your lack of wealth? Do you get angry about your financial situation? Are you always wishing you had more? Do you worry that things are never going to improve? If you answered yes to any of these questions then that is your cue to change the song you are playing. Remember your energy is your servant and it gives you only what you instruct it to.

Relationships

The people we are in relationship with are always a mirror, reflecting our own beliefs, and simultaneously we are mirrors, reflecting beliefs.

So relationship is one of the most powerful tools for growth...if we look honestly at our relationships we can see so much about how we have created them.

-Shakti Gawain. Creative Visualisation.

Many people seek a relationship, friendship, soul mate, twin-soul and/or to maintain such a relationship or union. Let's start with those who are lacking a relationship.

I have written earlier about those who are lacking a relationship and seeking one, and how they are blocking a relationship with their own energy. Some may truly believe they are a positive person and doing all the right things yet they remain single and looking for that special someone. If you give out the same energy all these years you are always going to get what you have always got.

As mentioned earlier, lack of a relationship is often due to someone putting out a negative energy or blocking with worrying; in this case about why they are still single and all their friends are not. People tell me that they are a positive person and ask why someone isn't in their life now. They often claim that they do all the right things. I notice the anxiety in those people, and the fact that they are impatient and demanding a relationship yesterday and worrying about their lack of relationship in their lives. I ask them who would be attracted to this kind of energy.

We need to look at this energy again that we are putting out toward relationships and also to being single. If you are complaining or moaning about what others have and you don't as in a relationship, then you are blocking a relationship from entering your life. The energy you are putting out with each complaint is telling your servant, your energy, that you actually don't want a relationship, you want more to complain about, and the result is you remain single and looking.

Take a really good, long look at yourself and your behaviour and the energy you put out, and ask yourself whether you would be attracted to this energy. If the answer is no or that you are not sure, then create a more attractive, active and positive energy.

If you are a single person you may have a void inside you that you need to fill because you are lonely; this void is not going to be filled by anyone coming into your life. You first need to find your own balance and centre in life and in yourself personally. This will free you of the void and it will draw someone into your life a lot faster than if you have a void. Don't take my word for it, try it and see what happens. When you do feel lonely or a void inside it is just a lack of balance and lack of energy in your life.

For those in a relationship who want to improve it, let's start with something really simple, that will make the world of difference in your relationship and maybe even improve other areas of your life too. Communication.

Do you feel that your partner doesn't hear you or maybe doesn't understand you as well as you would like? If your answer is yes, then you are not alone. This is very common in many relationships. So I will give you a brief lesson in improving the communication in your relationship and maybe your family.

I have observed many times how partners don't talk to one another; they talk at them or down to them. I have also noticed partners – even out in public – just yell at one another, put one another down, make jokes at the other's expense. If just these few sound familiar then ask yourself how you talk to your partner. Do you talk to them or at them? How would you feel if you were on the receiving end? Would it be something you would enjoy receiving yourself? Once you are more aware of how you are communicating with your partner ask yourself, now if I had someone speak to me like that, how would I like it?

I have noticed how many parents yell at their children in public. This gives me an insight into how they are spoken to at home, and maybe even how they treat their partners. I wonder how parents who yell at their children would like it if someone much bigger stood over and yelled at them. I suspect they would not like it at all, so why do it to their children?

If you are not aware of how you are communicating with and speaking to your partner and children, then the energy you are giving out is that you have given up on your relationship with them. To improve the situation and bring about positive improvements in your present or future relationships, be more aware of how you talk to people including your family and your partner, and ask yourself if I was on the receiving end of that would I like it?

Closely observing yourself and how you communicate and talk to other people including your partner may seem like a task at first, but after a time it will become very second nature. In no time at all you will be leading others by your example, including your partner.

It may take time to get this right. Don't be hard on yourself, as you are undoing many years of programming. Your partner is more than likely going to continue to act the same for a while after you start to change, as they don't know any different, so it is up to you to lead by example and gently educate your partner.

Soon you will feel listened to and heard and understood, as you are hearing your partner more and also listening to yourself. You have started reinvesting in your relationship, and the energy you have put out in this way will give you huge positive results.

To feel heard in your relationship, first start listening to yourself, as being aware of yourself may help you so much. If you are listening to yourself, then you are going to start putting this energy out and drawing this energy back in. As a result you may feel you are being heard more and understood more.

Also taking the time to listen to another and hearing them is also energy that is put out by you. Investing time in listening to some one is going to be rewarding for the person who feels listened to, but also very rewarding to you as you draw in an energy that is a lot more nurturing for you and your relationship.

To have awareness in your relationship is going to make you more present in your relationship, this is a more nurturing and caring energy to be investing into your relationship.

Investing time in yourself is going to also mean investing time into your relationship. As the more you learn about yourself and understand yourself, you will be a healthier and much more attractive energy to be with and to share time with, making for a much healthier and happier relationship.

Health

Pain and Suffering are a measure of your resistance to change.

So many people who are in a major life crisis suddenly fall seriously ill. A crisis in life is always a message to make a major change in your lifestyle, thinking, in your attitude, or in all of these and more.

A serious health crisis is a signal that you are resisting change in life. A heart attack is a very powerful way of saying that you have by passed your heart in your whole approach to life.

Now, suddenly, a heart by-pass is looming.

Move and flex with change. It is a regular feature in life, so you may as well learn to use it rather than resist it.

Michael J. Roads, The Oracle.

Health and making changes in your health is also up to you. It is a very sensitive subject as many who are ill are very attached to their illness or disease. It is like a part of them. To pick at someone's condition or state of health is to attack them; a bit like attacking their baby. People are often sensitive about their health and having illness healed as it has become like a limb and you are telling them to just cut it off. That would not seem like a wonderful idea for anyone. Letting go of a long-standing health condition needs a lot more understanding than just saying 'Let me heal you now.' to someone. Try to see their health condition from their point of view instead of yours.

Some people actually hide behind health conditions and illnesses, using them as their excuse for not moving forward in life. In such people, there may be fears that need addressing first before a healing of any kind can take place. These fears may be displayed as anger or frustration toward others or their condition. Understanding such emotions helps a great deal in removing the fears bringing about healing.

There are many levels of healing to go through on one's journey back to a healthy self. Using and understanding the methods within these pages will get you moving through these levels at whatever speed suits you best and you will find a much healthier you at the end of it.

You only get one chance this lifetime with your body and your health. How you treat yourself and your body today may come back around and help you or hinder you in the future.

The energy we put out about our health is very important and there are so many emotions one goes through with their health. You can either feed this emotion or you can let your emotions and feelings do their job and then release them. Feel your emotions but don't feed into them. Feeding into an emotion is you seeing the emotion and not letting it do its job. When you are feeding into it, you don't clear it and you create another emotional and/or energy block. Being able to learn from your emotions is an opportunity to heal yourself and help your condition.

It may not cure all health conditions completely but it may make you feel a lot more comfortable or more at ease than dis-eased.

When you feed an emotion it can become an energy block causing obstacles and even health problems. Feeding some emotions can even create toxins in your body that aggravate some health conditions.

Try a little understanding in your life and try to stay aware of what you feel. If you have to, write on a sticker and place it in your diary on every single page to remind you not to put yourself down, to be a little nicer to yourself or to stop feeding into your emotions. This is a start and will lead you to being more balanced and more empowered. With balance and empowerment comes clarity and an inner calm putting you in a stronger position to make positive changes to your life and your health.

Gaining understanding of yourself and your emotions is a great way to go about embracing changes to your health.

Realize that if you take what you have learnt in *Who Stole My Energy?* And apply it, then your health may very well improve. Are you ready for that? I have seen people use the methods in these pages and as a result their conditions have cleared up and they have found a method that works for them. But then once they realize they are not getting the attention they used to get, they no longer know how to communicate without doing so through their emotions. They omit to grieve for the past condition or the person they once were, and in many cases ill health recurs.

Healing brings about change. As with all change, one needs to be ready to let the person they once knew go; to say their farewells. Sometimes this is not an easy thing to do as it is like having to learn to walk and talk again. So gaining healing is one part of the journey. The other half of the journey is getting to know and welcoming the new person who has emerged, while saying goodbye to an old friend; the outgoing health condition.

If you are very healthy and there is absolutely nothing wrong with your health, then understanding yourself, your emotions and behavior as described in this book will maintain a stronger and healthier you. See this as a form of health maintenance like brushing or flossing your teeth; daily maintenance assuring you of a healthier you and a healthier life.

Understanding more about yourself can really help you on so many levels and in so many areas of your life. It really is that simple.

Weight Management

No matter what your thoughts are concerning your body, body consciousness is ceaselessly acting upon those thoughts.

When you look in the mirror do you like what you see? Do you think, "Oh wow, I really love this body of mine," or are your thoughts more critical?

Every criticism of your body is received by the cells of your body, and they act on this. You will grow 'toward' all that you criticize, simply because this is your focus.

Similarly, if you look in the mirror feeling a glow of pride and happiness in your body, this translates into good health and overall well-being.

All I am saying here is that your body and you are One. Focussed thought has a very powerful effect, either for the better or worse.

It's up to you!

— *Michael J. Roads, The Oracle.*

Change in all areas of your life is important but let's talk about one that seems to plague many people, and that is a change in your body weight. Your body weight can transform your life for the better or for the worse. Nowadays there are many weight loss systems, exercise machines and videos/DVD's and support programmes all pushing you to lose weight, and the thing is they can all work and they can all work really well. But how do we use these systems so we are working smarter and not harder?

A key way of doing so is to get honest with yourself and taking the steps to a healthier energy and a healthier emotional understanding. There are many reasons why people are overweight. They may be valid in your eyes and the eyes of society, but these reasons are excuses. These reasons are crutches to hide behind so you don't have to look at the problem. And the problem isn't your weight.

The problem is you eating whenever you have an emotional reaction, feel unsafe, feel lonely, are afraid of change, are angry and so on. You see the food and the weight is not the problem. The problem is you not wanting to deal with someone or something. That is what puts on the weight, it is keeping you overweight and makes you regain weight time and time again. Knock the problem – the need to emotionally eat – on the head and you knock gaining weight on the head at the same time.

Here is something to provoke your thoughts; before we talk further about emotion and what emotionally eating is. When something happens you do not feel an emotion first off, you actually have a thought first. You may have heard the phase *we are not our thoughts* and *we are not our thoughts because we choose our thoughts. So when something happens we choose a thought, and with this thought we choose an emotion, and then we choose an action, or choose if we will feed into this emotion, or choose to suppress this emotion with food. So we are not just suppressing an emotion but a thought as well.*

When you feel emotional or insecure or lonely or down for any reason, by not trying to understand the emotion, the rut you are in gets deeper and deeper. In the end it makes it seem all too difficult to lose weight, or to even try to get out of that rut.

You may feel trapped in the body you are in and trapped in your patterns of eating to cope with your emotions. If you are feeling trapped in your body you are most probably feeling lost in yourself and in life.

When you feel lost, you lack direction in life, and people without direction in life can feel frustrated, impatient, angry and vulnerable.

This is your opportunity to understand these emotions as they are going to lead you to your answers. So go back to the chapter on emotional behaviour and start understanding your emotions as a starting point. First realize your emotions have a job to do. Stop giving your power away to your emotions and regain some control of your life and your weight. It is your choice to take this step, take back your control and your power. You are in control of your thoughts and so you are in control of your emotions, it is your choice.

Nothing holds more power over the body than beliefs of the mind, and you are in control of your own thoughts and with these thoughts make choices about what you wish to manifest in create in your life.

The person you are today and the person you want to be are not worlds apart and over time you can bridge that gap. The time it will take you to bridge that gap is the time it will take you to read this book and take a step toward understanding yourself a little bit more. Then when you go and start a new exercise programme you will be working smarter and not harder.

We may see an overweight person and judge them as fat, lazy, unmotivated, or say they don't take pride in themselves or their bodies. Realize how you judge anyone is how you see yourself. You may be in shape, fit, toned and healthy but inside dwells your insecurities that you display for the whole world to see when you judge another person.

People who are overweight are not fat and lazy; they have found a way to cope with their emotions by using food to suppress their emotions. Many people have other coping strategies like using alcohol, drugs, cigarettes, being a workaholic, retail therapy, being a gym junkie and I am sure many others. Food taken as a result of emotional overeating and binge eating is just another coping strategy. All coping devices can be removed if you understand why you are using them.

If you are serious about losing weight, if you are serious about keeping that weight off, then get serious about getting to know you. Get serious about understanding who you are, understanding your emotions and understanding that you are putting out an energy that must be returned. It is all about working smarter not harder.

Who Stole My Energy is about giving you some added tools to add to your toolbox to help you achieve the rewards you want and deserve.

As you get to know yourself more and understand more about yourself, you are going to be clearing blocks from you and from your energy that is meant to flow through you unobstructed by blocks. When you start to remove your emotional blocks and energy blocks your body is going to naturally realign its self and as a result your body will start to balance its self out. As a result your weight will begin to balance its self out naturally. Rewarding you with the weight loss you may have desired, or an easier way to maintain your weight loss.

You may be equipped with a sensible diet, and a gym membership and maybe even a personal trainer to help you achieve your desired result. But if you take some time, not a lot of time, just a small investment of time to get to know yourself and take what is written with in these pages and start to use these tools to help yourself on a daily basis your weight loss will be a much easier goal to achieve. This is going to mean you work much smarter with a lot less effort, and reach results that you know you are going to be able to maintain with a little more ease.

Make life a little easier for yourself, make your weight loss and maintaining your weight loss a little more easier for you. Gain these rewards by investing just a little time in yourself. This is all about you and helping you gain the benefits and rewards you want.

Empowering You

The truth is that life is hard and dangerous; that he who seeks his own happiness does not find it; that he who is weak must suffer; that he who demands love, will be disappointed; that he who is greedy, will not be fed; that he who seeks peace, will find strife; that truth is only for the brave; that joy is only for him who does not fear to be alone; that life is only for the one who is not afraid to die.

—Joyce Carey

Take all that you have learnt from *Who Stole My Energy?* and make it work for you in the future. Life isn't hard. People make it that way and they truly do. You have a choice to continue to make life hard or to change it.

Many people talk about motivation and staying inspired in trying to reach goals. But sometimes this is not enough to keep people on their particular path so that they can reach their goal. If you take the knowledge in this book and your own understanding and awareness you will achieve your goals and it won't feel like punishment or you sacrificing so much anymore. It may even make achieving your goals a lot easier.

Don't take my word for it, try it yourself and know that wisdom is not learnt; it is experienced. So experience *Who Stole My Energy?* for yourself and from that, gain wisdom. With wisdom comes great clarity and balance. If you have clarity and balance you will see your path and be able to walk it.

You may stumble and fall at times but you will know that you have fallen. You will be able to pick yourself up, learn from the experience, gain the wisdom that comes with it and carry on purposefully.

If you are in the dark, you are not being aware, you are not being kinder to yourself and you are not trying to understand yourself. When you fall in the dark, you don't know why, and you can be there for a very long time seeking a right direction again. Use the tools of understanding and awareness to bring yourself into the light, to gain clarity so that you can see clearly enough where you are going to attain your goals.

Who Stole My Energy? is about taking back your control and your power. Through understanding and awareness you can achieve this. If you gain more insight into yourself and learn more about yourself you will become a magnet for all that you want in this life and all that you need. To truly know yourself is to be empowered and when you feel this power coarse through you then you will know that goals once unattainable to you seem more real and reachable.

Know life is nothing to be feared. It is just your reflection. You can know your own future by seeing the reflection in your life around you today. You are your greatest resource for gaining knowledge and answers, and so you hold the key to empowering yourself to make those changes and gaining success, happiness and goals that once seemed unreachable.

Everything that happens to us is a reflection of who we are.

Rewards

So you have made it to the end of *Who Stole My Energy* and or maybe you just rushed to the end of the book to see what rewards you can get from reading this work.

When you take the time to understand how energy infects your everyday life, in a good way and in a bad way you can make it work for you and as a result manifest and create a life you want to live instead of one you may have thought you had to put up with.

Energy comes in all forms – be it in the spoken word, in your actions, and even comes in the form of your thoughts. Think about this – if you are not aware of your thoughts and the mind chatter that goes on – when you go to sleep at night your body sleeps, your mind does not and continues to send out this energy. If you have taken the time to understand how energy is working for you or against you, then you can have more control over what comes into your life and what does not.

So with this new understanding about energy you can create the rewards you want – be them in your career, business, relationships, marriage, family and your health and well-being or in some other aspect of your life.

You even gain further rewards from learning more about your emotional behaviour, self talk and how you may be resisting and how this all effects you. Why is this so important?

When you are a young child you may want to drive a car, but you do not just jump into a car and know exactly what to do, and if you did you may cause damage or harm to yourself or others. When you are born you are not given a manual on how to live this life, no one gives you a blueprint to life, you have to do your best to make your way through to get where you believe you need to be. So *Who Stole Your Energy?* is here to give some assistance in getting to know you and your behaviours a little better, so you can gain a healthier and happier life for you, and so a more rewarding life for yourself.

Every single one of us is made up of energy, and if there are emotional blocks and/or energy blocks, blocking this flow of energy in the body, then blocks are what tend to manifest into ones reality. Blocks are created by a lack of understanding about yourself and how you can suppress so much of your feelings and emotions and more.

Remove some of these blocks with gaining a little more understanding about yourself and then the energy that flows through us will begin to free up and start to flow naturally again. As a result your body will start to realign itself and naturally balance its self out.

Then as a result of your body realigning its self everything in your body starts to balances itself out again, such as your body weight, and even help you manage your pain levels due to stress or a health condition.

Further, you gain a newfound clarity in your life that can help you see more clearly where you are going. For some people who may believe they are off path in life and have lost their direction gaining this clarity is like someone has shined a light on their path to show them the way. Maybe you are in Sales and you have a high target to reach and you may have thought once that is not possible, but now you have a newfound clarity and not so much cluttering your mind and thoughts and/or your life that you can see exactly where you are going. Putting you in a position to reap the rewards you want and need.

Many invest years in their education to be rewarded with the career or business they want, giving them a lifestyle they want. *Who Stole Your Energy?* is an investment into getting to know you so that you can enjoy the life you have, and enjoy the rewards you have worked hard for, and to enjoy the rewards that you may not have even realized were there before.

Taking the time to get to know you, that is what *Who Stole Your Energy?* is all about. The more you know about the vehicle you are travelling in, the better the chances are that you are going to get where you want to go, and with a lot more ease and comfort, and gain benefits and rewards in not only your professional life but your personal life.

Why get what you have always got? – when you can manifest and create so much more for yourself. Invest some time in you and reap the rewards that are waiting for you.

References

Baird, David. 2000. *A Thousand Paths to Wisdom.*

Published by MQ Publications Limited. 12 The
Ivories, 6-8 Northampton Street, London N1 2HY

ISBN: 1-84072-119-7

Baird, David. 2000. *A Thousand Paths to
Tranquillity.*

Published by MQ Publications Limited. 12 The
Ivories, 6-8 Northampton Street, London N1 2HY

ISBN: 1-84072-005-0

Blum, Ralph. 1982 *The Book of Runes.*

Published by Angus & Robertson Publishers

ISBN 0 207 15022 2

Browne, Sylvia. 2006. *If You Could See What I See.*

Published by Hay House, Inc. PO Box 5100,
Carlsbad,

California, USA. 92018-5100.

Chopra, Deepak M.D. 1993 *Ageless Body, Timeless Mind: A Companion Guide and Journal.*

Published by: Crown Arts & Letters, a division of Crown Publishers, Inc.,

201 East 50th Street, New York, New York, USA. 10022

ISBN: 0-517-59818-3

Emoto, Masaru. 2004 *The Hidden Messages in Water.*

Translated by David A. Thayne

Published by: Beyond Words Publishing Inc.

20827 N.W. Cornell Road, Suite 500

Hillsboro, Oregon 97124-9808

ISBN: 2004002415

Hayward, Susan.1985 *A Guide for the Advanced Soul.*

Published by: In-tune Books

PO Box 193

Avalon NSW 2107

Australia

ISBN: 0 9590439 3 4

Levin, Daniel. 2005. *The Zen Book.*

Published by Hay House, Inc. PO Box 5100, Carlsbad,

California, USA. 92018-5100.

Hardcover ISBN10: 1-4019-0875-6

Tradepaper ISBN 10: 1-4019-0701-6

Roads, Michael J. 2005. *The Oracle.*

Published by Roadslight Pty Ltd. PO Box 778
Nambour, Queensland 4560, Australia

ISBN 0 975847600

Millman, Dan. 1993. The Live You Were Born To Live

An H J Kramer Book Published in a joint venture with

New World Library.

ISBN: 0915811-60-X

Editorial office:

HJ Kramer Inc

PO Box 1082, Tiburon, CA 94920

Administrative office:

New World Library 14 Pamaron Way, Novato California 94949